A Sense of Story

A Sense of Story

Essays on Contemporary Writers for Children

by

John Rowe Townsend

J. B. LIPPINCOTT COMPANY
Philadelphia New York

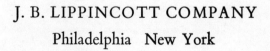

Library of Congress Catalog Card Number 79-155797
Printed and bound in England

Contents

Author Bibliographies

The bibliographies which follow each essay list the books of each author in order of publication. Both the British and American publishers of each title are cited, where appropriate, and, in each case, the publisher in the country of origin is stated first. All the major works of each writer are given and, in most cases, examples of their short stories for children are listed at the end of each bibliography.

The Author and Publishers are grateful to those authors, publishers and others who assisted with the compilation of the bibliographies.

Introduction

This book is an introduction to the work of nineteen leading English-language writers for children. It mixes American, British and Australian writers; it includes brief biographical details and notes by the authors on themselves and their books. But mainly it consists of a set of essays in which I have tried to consider their work in literary terms.

Surveys of children's books are numerous, and so are aids to book selection, but discussion at any length of the work of individual contemporary writers is scarce. Such discussion may be thought unnecessary. I know from conversations over a period of years that there are intelligent and even bookish people to whom children's literature, by definition, is a childish thing which adults have put away. Such people may have a personal or professional interest – it is useful to have some ideas on what books to give to their children or to read to a class – but they do not pretend to be interested on their own account, and regard such an interest as an oddity, an amiable weakness. It is not my intention to quarrel with them. We cannot all be interested in everything.

Yet children are part of mankind and children's books are part of literature, and any line which is drawn to confine children or their books to their own special corner is an artificial one. Wherever the line is drawn, children and adults and books will all wander across it. Long ago *Robinson Crusoe* and *Gulliver's Travels* were adopted as children's stories. Adults have taken over *Huckleberry Finn*, argue about *Alice*, and probably enjoy *The Wind in the Willows* as much as their children do. Dickens and other Victorian novelists wrote books for the whole family; Stevenson and Rider Haggard and John Buchan and Anthony Hope wrote for boys and grown-up boys alike; and it can be offered as a pseudo-Euclidean proposition that any line drawn between books for adults and books for children must pass through the middle of Kipling.

Arbitrary though it is, the division has become sharper in the present century. The main reasons have been the expansion of school and public libraries for children, and corresponding changes in the book trade. On the whole, I believe that the children's library has been a blessing to authors and publishers as well as children. The growth of a strong institutional market has eased some of the cruder commercial pressures and has made possible the writing and publication of many excellent books which otherwise could never appear. But it has hardened the dividing line between children's books and adult books into a barrier, behind which separate development now takes place.

Although the distinction is administrative rather than literary, it must have some effect on the way books are written. Yet authors are individualists, and still tend to write the book they want to write rather than one that will fit into a category. Arguments about whether such-and-such a book is 'really for children' are always cropping up, and are usually pointless in any but organizational terms. The only practical definition of a children's book today—absurd as it sounds—is 'a book which appears on the children's list of a publisher'.

Books are, in fact, continually finding their way on to the children's lists which, in another age, would have been regarded as general fiction. Abetted by their editors, writers for children constantly push out the bounds of what is acceptable. Yet because of the great division these writers, and their books, are probably more shut off than ever from the general public. (And, from this point of view, the probable growth of 'young adult' lists may raise still more fences and create new pens in which books can be trapped.) A minor reason for a book on contemporary writers for children could well be a sense of dissatisfaction with artificial barriers; a feeling that there are authors who deserve a wider public; a belief that many books which are good by any standard will now only be found by looking on the children's side of the line.

In fiction at least, the balance of talent has shifted sharply between adult books and children's books in recent years. Brian Jackson, director of the Advisory Centre for Education, in an essay on Philippa Pearce in *The Use of English* for Spring 1970, declared that 'ours is the golden age of children's literature'—a view with which I agree, although the figure of speech grows wearisome – and expressed surprise that 'the great outburst of children's books this last thirty years' should come about when there is no longer a sturdy adult literature to support it.

> Children's writing [he said] is a large and apparently self-contained genre, as it never was before. It is independent of the current adult novel. On the face of it, you wouldn't therefore expect its burgeoning richness. Could it be, ironically, that precisely because the adult novel is so weak in this country, some talents have been drawn into the children's field and flourished (as others have been drawn into scientific fiction and perished)?

The weakness of the current adult novel – which is not a solely British phenomenon, although it is more obvious here than in the United States – hardly needs to be demonstrated. Among much converging testimony, I draw almost at random from a few books and articles that come to hand. Anthony Burgess, in *The Novel Now* (1967), quotes Evelyn Waugh's view that 'the originators, the exuberant men, are extinct, and in their place subsists and mostly flourishes a generation notable for elegance and variety of contrivance'; and Burgess, while questioning the 'elegance' if not the 'variety of contrivance', adds on his own account: 'We cannot doubt that the twenty years since the Second World War have produced nothing to compare with the masterpieces of, say, the half-century before it.' Storm Jameson, in *Parthian Words* (1970), asks how many of us dip twice into 'the endless flow of social trivia, on its level interesting, which pours from the pens or typewriters of contemporary novelists'. The American novelist Isaac Bashevis Singer, writing in the *New York Times Book Review* on 9 November 1969, expressed the belief that 'while adult literature, especially fiction, is deteriorating, the literature for children is gaining in quality and stature'. Explaining why he began to write for children in his late years, Singer declared that the child in our time

> has become a consumer of a great growing literature – a reader who cannot be deluded by literary fads and barren experiments. No writer can bribe his way to the child's

attention with false originality, literary puns and puzzles, arbitrary distortions of the order of things, or muddy streams of consciousness which often reveal nothing but the writer's boring and selfish personality. I came to the child because I see in him a last refuge from a literature gone berserk and ready for suicide.

I am not sure that despair over the state of adult fiction is a good reason for becoming a writer for children. But I believe that the general picture of an ailing adult literature in contrast with a thriving literature for children is broadly correct and would be accepted by most people with knowledge of both fields. I do not mean to say that children's books are 'better' than adults', or to claim for them an excessively large place in the scheme of things. And I admit that plenty of rubbish is published for children – as indeed it is for grown-ups. But I am sure there are people writing for children today who are every bit as talented as their opposite numbers among writers for adults.

The reasons for the strength of modern fiction for children are too many and complex to be dealt with in part of a short introduction, but some of them can be hinted at. Adult fiction means, effectively, the novel. The novel is a recent form, and may be only a transitional one. Its heyday was the rapidly-changing but pre-electronic Victorian age. At present it gives the impression of shrinking into a corner: narrow, withdrawn, self-preoccupied. But children's literature has wild blood in it; its ancestry lies partly in the long ages of storytelling which preceded the novel. Myth, legend, fairy-tale are alive in their own right, endlessly reprinted, endlessly fertile in their influence. Modern children's fiction is permeated by a sense of story. Many writers, knowingly or unknowingly, return again and again to the old themes, often reworking them in modern or historical settings. And even where the children's novel runs parallel to its adult counterpart, there is often a freedom, speed and spontaneity which the adult novel now seems to lack.

This, I believe, is the result of an odd but happy paradox. On the one hand, most modern writers for children insist that they write, with the blessing of their editors, the books they want to write for their own satisfaction. The classic statement of this position was made by Arthur Ransome in a letter to the editor of *The Junior Bookshelf* as long ago as 1937: 'You write not for children but for yourself, and if, by good fortune, children enjoy what you enjoy, why then, you are a writer of children's books... No special credit to you, but simply thumping good luck.' C. S. Lewis said that the only reason why he would ever write for children was 'because a children's story is the best art form for something you have to say'; he also remarked that 'I am almost inclined to set it up as a canon that a children's story which is enjoyed only by children is a bad children's story'. Yet anyone writing a book that will appear on a children's list must be aware of a potential readership of children. This is the fruitful contradiction from which the children's writer benefits. However much he is writing for himself he must, consciously or unconsciously, have a special sense of audience. As Arthur Ransome, rightly unworried by any inconsistency, went on to say in the letter already quoted: 'Every writer wants to have readers, and than children there are no better readers in the world.'

An author can – as I have said elsewhere – expect from the reading child as much intelligence, as much imagination, as from the grown-up, and a good deal more readiness to enter into things and live the story. He can take up his theme afresh as if the world were new, rather than picking it up where the last practitioner let it drop and allowing for the weariness and satiety of his readers. He cannot expect children to put up with long-windedness or pomposity or emperors' clothes; but that is a discipline rather than a restriction. True, the child's range of experience is limited. There are still some kinds of book that are not likely to appear on the children's list: not because they will corrupt a child but because they will bore him. But, in general, children and their books are much less inhibited now than they were in Arthur Ransome's day. In my experience, children's writers do not feel much hampered; mostly they are able to do what they want to do. They are fortunate people. Their sense on the one hand of scope and freedom, on the other of a constantly-renewed and responsive readership, freshens their work and makes this an exhilarating sector to be concerned with.

Nevertheless, children's books need to be appraised with coolness and detachment, simple enthusiasm being little better than simple unawareness. A critical approach is desirable not only for its own sake but also as a stimulus and discipline for author and publisher, and – in the long run – for the improvement of the breed. This indeed is the strongest reason for it. Donnarae MacCann, introducing a series of articles in the *Wilson Library Bulletin* for December 1969, quoted from Henry S. Canby's *Definitions*:

> Unless there is somewhere an intelligent critical attitude against which the writer can measure himself . . . one of the chief requirements for good literature is wanting . . . The author degenerates.

In the United States and Britain, the positions of writers for children in the league-table are well known among specialists in the field; possibly too well known. But, as Donnarae MacCann says, 'there is no body of critical writing to turn to, even for those books which have been awarded the highest literary prizes in children's literature in Britain and America'. Of the authors discussed in this book, only a few have been the subject of any sustained critical appraisal. The children's writer, when his work begins to make any impression, can expect his new book to get a few reviews: some by specialists with much knowledge but little critical acumen, some by non-specialists with – presumably – critical acumen but not much knowledge of children's books, some by people with no obvious qualifications at all. With luck the book may be reviewed in two or three places by critics who can place it in its context and can exercise some worthwhile judgment; but they are unlikely to have much space in which to work. And reviewing, even at its best, is a special and limited form of criticism: a rapid tasting rather than a leisurely consideration.

Mention of the criticism of children's books will usually lead to an argument about the relevance of various criteria. It seems to me that it is perfectly possible to judge books for children by non-literary standards. It is legitimate to consider the social or moral or psychological or educational impact of a book; to consider how many children, and what kind of children, will like it. But it is dangerous to do this and call it criticism. Most disputes over standards are fruitless because the antagonists suppose their criteria to be mutually exclusive; if one is right the other must be wrong. This is not necessarily so. Different kinds of assessment are valid for different purposes. The important thing is that everyone should understand what is being done.

The critic who is concerned with a book as literature cannot, however, carry his 'standards' around with him like a set of tools ready for any job. He should, I believe, approach a book with an open mind and respond to it as freshly and honestly as he is able; then he should go away, let his thoughts and feelings about it mature, turn them over from time to time, consider the book in relation to others by the same author and by the author's predecessors and contemporaries. If the book is for children he should not let his mind be dominated by the fact; but neither, I think, should he attempt to ignore it. Myself—as one who remembers being a child, has children of his own, and has written for children—I could not, even if I wished, put children out of my mind when reading books intended for them. Just as the author must, I believe, write for himself yet with awareness of an audience of children, so the critic must write for himself with an awareness that the books he discusses are books written for children.

But this awareness should not, I think, be too specific. Neither author nor critic should be continually asking himself questions such as: 'Will this be comprehensible to the average eleven-year-old?' We all know there is no average child. Children are individuals, and will read books if they like them and when they are ready for them. A suggestion that a book may appeal to a particular age-group or type of child can be helpful, especially in reviews, but it should always be tentative and it should not affect one's assessment of merit. It has always seemed clear to me that a good book for children must be a good book in its own right. And a book can be good without being immensely popular and without solving its readers' problems or making them kinder to others.

It may seem that in these remarks about the criticism of children's literature I am by implication making highflown claims for the book that follows. It is not so. I am fully aware of my shortcomings. In saying what I think can and should be done, I am not suggesting that I have done it. And the dual aim of introducing writers to a wider public and addressing myself seriously to their work has set some problems of its own. Nineteen authors may seem a small number to pick out from all the talented people now writing for children in English, but is quite a large number for one person to study. To be properly equipped to write a 2,000-word essay on an author, one should be qualified to write a whole book on him, for the knowledge and understanding required are no less. I know all too well that I have not qualified myself to write nineteen books.

The writers included here are not presented with any claim that they are 'the best'. Every reader with knowledge of the field will be irritated, if not outraged, by my omissions, and probably by some of my inclusions. Everyone will feel that some writers who are left out are better than some who are in. I would not try to deny it. I have chosen on a personal basis. These are authors whose work particularly interests me and about whom I feel I have something to say. There have, however, been factors at work other than purely individual inclination. 'Contemporary' is a key word in the selection; I have chosen writers who are alive and active at the time of going to press. I have tried to produce a reasonable mixture of American, Australian and British authors while confining myself to those whose work is known and available in all three countries. This causes no injustice to British or Australian writers, for American publishers are assiduous in seeking out and buying rights in their work; but it is hard on some good American writers whose work is unknown or little known over here. The temptation to list authors whom I should have liked to include, but for one reason or another could not, is strong but must be resisted. It could not make the process of selection less invidious.

My thanks are due to all the publishers who have helped me with books and information, and to all the authors who have been kind enough either to write specially for me about themselves and their work or to give permission for the use of extracts from lectures and articles. It will be seen that their contributions differ a good deal from each other. This is because of differences in my own approaches to them. I did not ask, or want, them all to do the same thing. If the resulting variety is a fault – though I do not think it is – the blame is mine.

Knutsford July 1970. J.R.T.

Joan Aiken

Joan Aiken was born in Rye, Sussex, in 1924, the daughter of the American writer Conrad Aiken. She married at nineteen; her husband, a journalist, died when she was thirty and her two children were five and three. She worked for six years on a magazine and for a year with a big advertising agency before becoming a full-time writer. Her home is a former inn at Petworth, Sussex. Her books include The Wolves of Willoughby Chase *(1962)*, Black Hearts in Battersea *(1964)*, Night Birds on Nantucket (*1966*), *and* The Whispering Mountain *(1968), which won the* Guardian *award for children's fiction and was a runner-up for the Carnegie Medal.*

Joan Aiken is one of the liveliest and most exuberant of today's writers for children. She is also one of the hardest to assess, for she has few points of resemblance to anyone else. She is an original, a writer who has marked out a special territory of her own.

For children at least, her appeal is primarily as a storyteller of great pace and resource. But she is a storyteller whose invention is peculiarly uninhibited; her plots are so wild and whirling, her disregard for probability so outrageous as to be highly enjoyable to some tastes while much less acceptable to others. At the same time, she is a humorist of individual flavour; and humour, too, is notoriously a matter of taste. If therefore, as I do, one responds wholeheartedly to her work, the response tends to be personal and spontaneous, appreciative rather than critical, and not easily susceptible to analysis.

Up to 1970, Miss Aiken has written – in addition to books for adults – four novels for children and four collections of short stories. The novels are all based on a single curious premise: that the Hanoverian succession to the throne of England never happened. It is the realm of unhistory, with Good King James III as the reigning monarch and the Hanoverians plotting to overthrow him in favour of Bonnie Prince Georgie:

> My Bonnie lies over the North Sea
> My Bonnie lies over in Hanover,
> My Bonnie lies over the North Sea,
> Oh why won't they bring that young man over?

The time is the early nineteenth century, and there are wolves and wild boar in the remoter parts of Britain; the wolves were driven by hard winters in Russia and northern Europe to migrate through the recently opened Channel Tunnel. Clearly, in such circumstances, anything can happen. There is no out-and-out magic in these stories, but the merest of lip service is paid to the laws of nature. A railway passenger has no difficulty in stabbing a wolf with a sliver of glass from a carriage window, or an inventor in devising a cannon that will fire across the Atlantic.

The first three novels – *The Wolves of Willoughby Chase, Black Hearts in Battersea,* and *Night Birds on Nantucket* – are loosely linked together and have characters in common. In the first, which is set in the frozen north of England, two small girls, left in the care of a wicked governess, are put into a brutally and parsimoniously run charity school, but duly escape to take part in the defeat of villainy. The second book is a story of deep, dark Hanoverian plotting, centred upon the London seat of the Duke of Battersea. In the third, the scene shifts to the eastern seaboard of America, from which Hanoverians are planning to blow up St James's Palace, complete with His Stuart Majesty. The fourth book, *The Whispering Mountain*, stands somewhat apart; it is set in the same imaginary period but has a Welsh background and concerns the recovery of a lost and legendary golden harp.

These are stories of eye-defeating speed and complexity which carry the reader breathlessly onward from page to page. There is no time to stop and consider probabilities; and indeed any writer of a rapid-action adventure story, even without the open licence which Joan Aiken has written for herself, faces less exacting standards of probability than does the realistic novelist. The two kinds of book run in different gears, and episodes are acceptable in one that would be quite unconvincing in the other. Yet a price must be paid for the high-speed storyteller's freedom of action, and it is in the portrayal of character. Character development in depth is a process of slow unfolding; the tempo is not the same. Miss Aiken commonly draws her characters with a few swift strokes; sometimes hardly draws them at all. When Miss Slighcarp, the newly-arrived governess in *The Wolves of Willoughby Chase*, snatches up a heavy marble hairbrush and strikes a savage blow at the maid who innocently picked up her private papers, we immediately know all we need to know about her. Both she and her brother—who appears in *Night Birds on Nantucket*—are double-dyed villains, and that is that.

Joan Aiken is, in fact, a caricaturist and a mimic. She catches a likeness and presents it in exaggerated form so that it is clear and recognizable—in the way in which a cartoonist's figures are clear and recognizable—by the exploitation of a salient feature. Because she works in words, the salient feature is usually a way of speech. Again and again her minor characters are defined by their idiosyncrasies of language. In *The Whispering Mountain* two Cockney rogues, Bilk and Prigman, speak entirely in thieves' cant:

> 'Watch out, Bilk, you silly cullion! Don't raise such a garboil, or we'll have half the macemongers in town on our tail.'

And there is an Oriental potentate, the Seljuk of Rum, who seems to have learned his English from a thesaurus:

> 'Doubtless you are wishing me at Jericho, Timbuktu, the ends of the earth, so I shall hasten to be off, take my departure, make myself few and far between, ho, ho! I have had a most pleasant, famous natter, gossip, conversazione with your good papa.'

Then, in *Night Birds on Nantucket*, there is the innocent inventor of the transatlantic cannon, Professor Axeltree Breadno, with his fractured middle-European English:

> 'Aha, konigsbang! Is soon blowing up London . . . Monsterbang, grosseboom . . . Is shooting up palast—Sint Jim's Palast, not?'

All this is, of course, shamelessly overdone; but it is not merely verbal high jinks, it is a kind of cartooning in words.

With Miss Aiken's gift for mimicry and caricature goes a tendency to burlesque. It would be misleading to describe her novels as parodies of earlier fiction, but there are elements of parody in them nonetheless. *The Wolves of Willoughby Chase* and *Black Hearts in Battersea* can be seen in one light as comic Victorian melodramas. *Night Birds on Nantucket* has in it something of a light, and light-hearted, skit on *Moby Dick*, for one of its main characters, Captain Casket, is the strange, sad skipper of a New Bedford whaler, obsessed with the pursuit of the pink whale Rosie. And *The Whispering Mountain* looks suspiciously like a send-up of all those children's stories in which elaborate riddles from the past are ingeniously unravelled.

There is a high Dickensian colour about the first two books which reminds one that Dickens, too, was, among other things, a mimic and a caricaturist. Although Joan Aiken does not for a moment attempt to be a writer of comparable weight, it seems clear that Dickens has been a major source of inspiration. Possibly he is master and victim at once, since much of his work could be described as Victorian melodrama and is part of the material she seems to be parodying. Mrs Brisket and her charity school in *The Wolves of Willoughby Chase* and the Twite household in *Black Hearts in Battersea* could have come straight from the Dickens stockpot. It is a curious literary relationship.

Miss Aiken has, in fact, several Dickensian qualities whose appearance is not restricted to the first two books. Like Dickens, she loves to work with a crowded canvas and can always find room for more figures, more detail, more action. Like him, she can evoke the physical presence of places and people; like his, though on a slighter scale, her more successful characters can be basically 'flat' and yet memorable, vivid, larger than life. And where she has the time or inclination to use more than her few quick strokes she can produce portraits of impressive power. Here is the bad Lord Malyn, villain of *The Whispering Mountain*:

> He was a tall man, not yet much past middle age. Seen close to, almost everything about him appeared pale—his fine thin lips were colourless, so was his skin. His hair looked as if it had been bleached by weather or ill-health. His long delicate hands were whiter than the lace ruffles

> which fell over them. Only his eyes had colour – they were a deep, clear, burning yellow, like the eyes of a tiger, dark-rimmed, with pupils small as peppercorns. He held a long, slender but heavy piece of gold chain, and played with it, pouring it from one hand to the other . . . It was an odd characteristic of Lord Malyn that, although he always appeared fatigued, he never seemed able to keep still, but was in continual, languid, restless motion; whereas Mr Hughes, with a sailor's economy of effort, moved only when it was needful, and then in a brisk, neat, finished manner.

From one point of view it is disappointing that we never really learn any more of Lord Malyn than we know after reading this; his part in the book is purely functional. But in this splendid portrait he is not only present in the flesh; we have the sense of a complicated man underneath.

Miss Aiken's young heroes and heroines are not particularly interesting. Some of her child characters, like Sylvia and Bonnie in *The Wolves of Willoughby Chase* and Dutiful Penitence in *Night Birds on Nantucket*, are little more than 'types'. The incredibly resourceful Owen of *The Whispering Mountain* appears to be a caricature of the standard juvenile hero; one cannot really care about him or doubt that he will come out on top. But Dido Twite, the sharp, shrewish, knowing child who appears first in *Black Hearts in Battersea*, then in *Night Birds on Nantucket*, is different. Gradually one comes to realize that, besides the Cockney perkiness which is immediately obvious, she has a heart and a genuine individuality. It is as though the author had come to care for her as she went along, and had breathed life into her. She is the most rounded and the most successful of Miss Aiken's child characters.

Joan Aiken is, I think, essentially a lightweight writer; and there is nothing wrong with that. Lightweights of quality are scarce. She is something more than a 'mere' entertainer, for the sheer imaginative stretch of her work must in itself have some liberating effect; the child who reads these novels must experience some widening of its own imaginative range. But I can see no moral or psychological complexities in her books; nor do they try to convey any view of life more subtle than that of the ordinary decent person. Good is good and bad is bad, and there is never any doubt which is which. And, reassuringly, good always triumphs in the end.

I cannot find any clear line of development in the first three novels, though there are differences of flavour. *The Wolves of Willoughby Chase* has a deliberate artlessness which the later books seem less concerned to maintain. *Black Hearts in Battersea* is the funniest of the books, and has some of the most splendid incidental details. (The eccentric fourth Duke of Battersea, we learn, spent a lifetime building Battersea Castle in pink granite in the shape of a half-open rose. When at last it was complete, he drove out to survey the effect. '"It looks like a cod cutlet covered in shrimp sauce," he said, drove home, took to his bed, and died.') *Night Birds on Nantucket* seems slightly less satisfactory, perhaps because Miss Aiken, in spite of her American and Canadian ancestry, is a very English writer, and her work does not quite transplant successfully. But she always has a trick or two in hand. Unpretentious but pleasant verses are a feature of this book, and she shows that she can turn a neat stanza:

> Oh fierce is the Ocean and wild is the Sound,
> But the isle of Nantucket is where I am bound.
> Sweet isle of Nantucket, where grapes are so red
> And the light flashes nightly on Sankaty Head.

The Whispering Mountain takes the proliferation of character and action as far, one would think, as it can go. It is so crowded that even an attentive reader forgets who all the people are and cannot grasp all that is happening. It is a feast; but possibly enough would have been as good. I feel that Miss Aiken will have to thin down the mixture a little. But if she does it will certainly not be through any shortage of ideas. Besides her novels she has written four books of short stories for children—*All You've Ever Wanted* (1953), *More Than You Bargained For* (1955), *A Small Pinch of Weather* (1969), and, for younger children, *A Necklace of Raindrops* (1968)—all of which make reckless use, in a chapter or even in a single page, of enough material to last many writers through a whole book.

Where extravagance is of the essence, it is hard to draw the line beyond which a writer is to be regarded as *too* extravagant.

Joan Aiken

To say that Joan Aiken often develops an idea or situation beyond reasonable limits, makes her characters behave absurdly, and indulges in wild excesses of word-play is not necessarily to make an adverse criticism. It could be retorted that these are exactly the things she sets out to do and that make her work what it is. And if the snaffle and the curb are not much in evidence, at least there is no doubt about the presence of the horse. Energy, speed, inventiveness, a gift for mimicry, a total command over words and, not least, a reckless audacity: it all adds up to a formidable array of qualities, and indicates why Joan Aiken can get away with ventures that the majority of sensible authors would never even attempt.

Joan Aiken writes:

I was born in England because my parents, respectively American and Canadian, had come to England shortly before, believing the education over here would be better for my elder brother and sister. I myself didn't get to school till I was twelve; by this time my parents were divorced and we were living with my mother, now married to English writer Martin Armstrong, in a very remote Sussex village. My mother, who has degrees from Radcliffe and McGill, taught me herself. This period was immensely formative; we read aloud all the time, and I read to myself. The house was full of books and there was no one much to play with; my elder brother and sister were off at boarding school and college, my half-brother was seven years younger. I used to tell him long stories on walks, and of course writing was a habit in our family with both father and stepfather in the business. From the age of five on, I kept a notebook of poems and stories, and Martin used to give me his cast-off typed sheets and royalty statements to write on. His criticisms and advice have always been splendid.

At sixteen I had my first acceptance: some poems taken by a magazine called *Abinger Chronicle*, run by Sylvia Sprigge, E. M. Forster and Max Beerbohm. I actually had the poems sent back with Beerbohm's comments scribbled on them in pencil balloons: '*Must* you rhyme home with foam?' he wrote. Encouraged by Martin, I sent some fairytales to the BBC, who did one on Children's Hour when I was seventeen. It was called *Yes, but Today is Tuesday*, and was included in my first collection, which Cape published in 1953. By that time I'd been married nine years, worked six years at the United Nations' London office, and had two children; I'd kept writing on and off but hadn't had a lot of time.

Publication of that first collection, *All You've Ever Wanted,* got me started seriously. I did another collection of children's short stories, *More Than You Bargained For*. The year after it came out my husband died, and it was necessary to get a job. I worked for six years on the magazine *Argosy*, where I learned a huge amount about practical writing. I did a year as an advertising copywriter with J. Walter Thompson, then left to write full-time. (I'd finished *The Wolves of Willoughby Chase* in my last year, part-time, at *Argosy*.) *Wolves* got a wonderful review in *Time* and began selling very well in the United States; ironically, I'd begun it in 1954 when my husband fell ill, and had to put it by.

I feel I've had an unusual lot of luck in my writing career; *two* lots of encouraging parents and unrivalled opportunities for reading when young. I think reading aloud is tremendously important. I've read a lot to my own children, including my own books in instalments as I wrote them. Their criticisms were very useful. Reading aloud shows up the faults very plainly; it's a most instructive process.

I suppose one ought to have theories about writing for children, but with me the theories seem to come second to the writing. However, thinking it over, what I believe is that children's books should never minimize the fact that life is tough; virtue ought to triumph in the end, because even the best-regulated children's lives are so insecure that they need reassurance, but there's no point in pretending that wickedness and hardship don't exist. And one should never, never write down to a hypothetical children's level or reduce one's vocabulary, and one should be very painstaking over the accuracy of details, which are what children notice particularly. But I'm sure, really, that the main thing is just to shove all theories aside and enjoy the writing; that's the only way to produce good work.

Joan Aiken

Bibliography

Novels for children:

THE KINGDOM AND THE CAVE. Abelard-Schumann, 1957.

THE WOLVES OF WILLOUGHBY CHASE. Jonathan Cape, 1962; Doubleday, 1963.

BLACK HEARTS IN BATTERSEA. Jonathan Cape, 1966; Doubleday, 1964.

NIGHT BIRDS ON NANTUCKET. Jonathan Cape, 1966; Doubleday, 1966.

THE WHISPERING MOUNTAIN. Jonathan Cape, 1968; Doubleday, 1969.

NIGHT FALL. Macmillan (*Topliner series*), 1969; Holt, Rinehart and Winston, 1970.

THE CUCKOO TREE. Jonathan Cape, 1971; Doubleday, 1971.

Collections of stories for children:

ALL YOU'VE EVER WANTED. Jonathan Cape, 1953.

MORE THAN YOU BARGAINED FOR. Jonathan Cape, 1955; Abelard-Schuman, 1957.

A NECKLACE OF RAINDROPS. Jonathan Cape, 1968; Doubleday, 1969.

ARMITAGE, ARMITAGE, FLY AWAY HOME. Doubleday, 1968.

A SMALL PINCH OF WEATHER. Jonathan Cape, 1969.

SMOKE FROM CROMWELL'S TIME. Doubleday, 1970.

THE KINGDOM UNDER THE SEA. Jonathan Cape, 1971.

ALL AND MORE. Jonathan Cape, 1971. (Stories which first appeared in *All You've Ever Wanted* and *More Than You Bargained For*.)

In addition to stories in the collections listed above, Joan Aiken's short stories include *The Dark Streets of Kimball's Green* in THE FRIDAY MIRACLE AND OTHER STORIES, edited by Kaye Webb (Puffin Books, 1969), *The Boy With A Wolf's Foot* in MAGPIE BOOK OF STORIES (Purnell, 1969), *The Palace Pigs* in ALLSORTS 3, edited by Ann Thwaite (Macmillan, 1970), *The Rose of Puddle Fratum* in THE WORLD OF BALLET, edited by Anne Geraghty (Collins, 1970), *The Lost Five Minutes* in ALLSORTS 4, edited by Anne Thwaite (Macmillan, London, 1971) and *A Long Day Without Water* in YOUNG WINTER'S TALES 2, edited by M. R. Hodgkin (Macmillan, London, 1971).

L. M. Boston

L. M. Boston was born at Southport, Lancashire, in 1892. She went to a boarding school in southern England, then to finishing school in Paris, and finally to Oxford to read English, which she cut short for service in a French hospital in World War I. She married an officer in the Royal Flying Corps and had one son, Peter Boston, who has illustrated most of her books and whom she has described as 'the original Tolly'. In the late 1930s she lived mainly on the Continent, returning to England and buying the manor house at Hemingford Grey, Huntingdonshire, in 1939. This house, where she has lived ever since, is the original of Green Knowe. Mrs Boston became a writer at the age of sixty; her principal books are the 'Green Knowe' novels and The Sea Egg. *She won the Carnegie Medal with* A Stranger at Green Knowe *(1961).*

'All my water is drawn from one well,' Lucy Boston said in a talk to the Children's Book Circle (an extract from which follows this essay). 'I am obsessed by my house . . . It is in the highest degree a thing to be loved.'

The manor at Hemingford Grey, disguised only in name as Green Knowe, dominates all her principal books except *The Sea Egg*, and could be said to be their central character. Her novels explore the house, partly as children might explore it, with a sense of discovery which in Mrs Boston has stayed fresh through the years, and partly in the way an artist will explore and re-explore a theme that engages his mind. And her explorations have been four-dimensional, for the house is many centuries old and full of the past: the tangible stone and wood and handed-down treasures; the intangible memories and presences.

In Mrs Boston's first two books for children – *The Children of Green Knowe* (1954) and *The Chimneys of Green Knowe* (1958) – a small boy named Tolly is staying at the house with his great-grandmother, who is significantly named Mrs Oldknow and who sometimes seems to blend with Mrs Boston herself. She tells him stories of children who have lived there in former times. And he encounters the children himself: whether in 'reality' or in an imagination shared with Mrs Oldknow is best left as an open question. In the first book, the children from the past are Toby, Alexander and Linnet, who all died in the Great Plague of 1665. In the second, they are blind Susan – the daughter of a Captain Oldknow who owned Green Knowe at the end of the eighteenth century and built a much grander house for his demanding wife around the old one – and Susan's friend-and-servant Jacob, the little black boy whom Captain Oldknow bought for her in Barbados.

The three later 'Green Knowe' books differ sharply from these and from each other. In *The River at Green Knowe* (1959), there is a change of cast. Mrs Oldknow and Tolly are not there; Green Knowe has been rented for the summer to the eccentric scientist Dr Maud Biggin and her friend Sybilla Bun who loves food and cookery. Dr Biggin's great-niece Ida and two displaced children, Oskar from Poland and Ping from China, come to stay with her. They set out to explore the river and make charts of their explorations. The river, smooth and sleepy on summer evenings, yet wilful and dangerous at times, flows through the heart of the story, and to some extent takes the central place occupied by the house in the previous two books. The Chinese boy Ping reappears, staying with Mrs Oldknow, in *A Stranger at Green Knowe* (1961) – the stranger is a gorilla that has escaped from a zoo and is befriended by Ping – and again in *An Enemy at Green Knowe* (1964), in which the house and its inhabitants are threatened by Dr Melanie D. Powers, a witch possessed by a demon lord.

The action of the 'Green Knowe' stories is often dramatic, sometimes melodramatic. It is not for their plots that the books stand out. The first two – *The Children of Green Knowe* and *The Chimneys of Green Knowe* – have an awkward box-within-a-box construction. Discoveries from the past, such as the family jewels in *Chimneys* and an ancient book of magic in *Enemy*, are too easy and perhaps too obvious. The long arm of coincidence makes unlikely sweeps. Some of the action in *River* and in *Enemy* lacks credibility even in its own terms. Only in *A Stranger at Green Knowe*, which brings Hanno the gorilla to this quiet corner of England, is the story as such both audacious and successful.

Nor is Mrs Boston remarkable as a creator of human characters. Most of her people are simply good or bad in varying degree; they have their place in the moral spectrum and do not depart from it. Tolly is a nice, polite small boy with a reserve of quiet courage; and so, precisely, is the Chinese boy Ping. Of all the child characters, only the blind girl Susan in the 'inner' story of *Chimneys* seems to me to be memorable; of the adults, none except Mrs Oldknow herself goes far beyond adequacy. Dr Melanie D. Powers, who threatens the house and the whole way of life in *Enemy*, is not even adequate: she is a silly, false and vulgar creature who cannot be taken too seriously and is never credibly imbued with the towering evil which the plot demands of her.

Mrs Boston is not, then, in my view particularly well endowed with the standard equipment of the novelist: the ability to create characters and tell a story about them. Even so, she is a writer of distinction. To start with, she has an excellent ear and uses the English language superbly. She can be poetic and evocative, as when Tolly returns to Green Knowe at the beginning of *Chimneys*, at a time when 'the wide and wandering garden was silky with daffodils'. But she is also strong, sharp and exact; and her style is perfectly suited to the Green Knowe setting. She is a highly intelligent writer and does not disguise it. Her sense of the past is subtle and haunting. There is deep feeling in her work, too; and she can go to the farther bounds of sentiment without taking the last, false step that would cross the brink into sentimentality. Here are Tolly and Mrs Oldknow, in the ancient house at evening, hearing a woman's voice softly singing a cradle song:

> 'Why are you crying, Granny? It's lovely,' [says Tolly.]
>
> 'It is lovely, only it is such a long time ago. I don't know why that should be sad, but it sometimes seems so.'
>
> The singing began again.
>
> 'Granny,' whispered Tolly again with his arm through hers, 'whose cradle is it? Linnet is as big as I am.'

'My darling, this voice is much older than that. I hardly know whose it is. I heard it once before at Christmas.'

It was queer to hear the baby's sleepy whimper only in the next room, now, and so long ago. 'Come, we'll sing it too,' said Mrs Oldknow, going to the spinet. She played, but it was Tolly who sang alone while, four hundred years ago, a baby went to sleep.

Most remarkably, Mrs Boston combines sensuousness with an unusual degree of empathy. A comparison with D. H. Lawrence – especially the Lawrence of the poems – is not as absurd as it may seem. She offers a strong sense of the natural world, living and breathing, to be seen through the alert eye and felt through the fingertips. It is this sensuous awareness that she feels to be precious in children, that she wishes to share with them, and that may have led her to write for them. In *Chimneys* she takes us with total conviction and involvement into the world of blind Susan, so largely perceived by touch; and then she shows us Tolly blindfolded, finding out for himself what it is like to be without sight. And after he has taken off the blindfold, Tolly lies back in the sun, exploring another aspect of Susan's world:

'Now I'll lie here and listen to what Susan heard,' he thought, and at once realized how much wind there was, and how big, tell-tale and friendly. It bumped into and passed round sheds, it crossed the gravel, bowling protesting dead leaves before it. It made a different sound in each tree, in some like the sea, in others like fretted tissue paper. How it whirled the yew branches about! Tolly could imagine the clouds moving like ships under full sail, but Susan would know nothing about clouds or sky, and never could. But surely somehow she would feel the *size* of the wind? She could hear it approach from far away and the immense hubbub of its passing. The birds were trying to sing, because it was March, but the song was interrupted, jerked out of their throats as they were tossed off the branches and flew with an extra flutter that reminded Tolly of rowing in rough water. He heard the branches of two trees that leaned against each other squeaking and groaning like an overloaded cart. He heard the Church clock strike one, and

> Boggis slipped past on his bicycle almost as quietly as an owl. The sound was so slight he opened his eyes to see if he had guessed right.

Soon afterwards comes the entry of a related Boston theme. Tolly climbing a great beech tree, finds that Susan, blind as she was, has climbed it before him. It was important to her as it is important to him. Susan's wise father and Tolly's wise grandmother understand that children must climb high and free, and do not prevent them from taking the risk.

Mrs Boston is not an explicitly moral writer, but her values are clearly to be seen. She believes in the goodness of the natural living creature, in roots, in continuity; and she is able to symbolize these values in the house, itself built of natural materials, which she has said she cannot think of as 'a thing'. She hates concrete and all it stands for. These values and the gift of empathy helped her to carry out the *tour-de-force* of *A Stranger at Green Knowe*. At first sight it seems incongruous to introduce a dangerous wild creature from the jungle into a quiet English countryside setting. Yet this clash and its resolution give the book its power, for out of striking dissonances a striking unity is achieved. And within Mrs Boston's frame of values the elements are not so incongruous after all. The gorilla and Green Knowe are both, in different ways, antitheses of the artificial urban civilization represented by the zoo. Moreover, Mrs Boston is able to lead us into the difficult but necessary act of identification with Hanno: we feel we know what it is like to have been born in the jungle and to be now in a cage; we believe fiercely that a few days of freedom are worth the sacrifice of a life in captivity.

Mrs Boston has written two books for younger children, both concerned with houses and both having clear family relationships with the 'Green Knowe' stories. In *The Castle of Yew* (1965), two boys, Joseph and Robin, enter an old lady's magic garden and are able by passionate longing to shrink themselves enough to inhabit a castle which is part of a chess game cut out of yew bushes. This is a book for, possibly, seven- to nine-year-olds; for younger children still Mrs Boston has written the text of a picture-book, *The House That Grew* (1969), about a tiny house, soft as a mushroom, that appeared in an orchard and got bigger and bigger. I do not myself feel that either of these books is successful. Mrs Boston seems to be consciously 'writing down' and not employing the qualities that make her the writer she is. Young children's books, I suspect, are not her true medium.

The Sea Egg (1967), her one remaining book for children up to the time of writing, is greatly different from the rest in subject and setting. She herself (in the talk already mentioned) has spoken of 'the flight to *The Sea Egg*', implying that it resulted from the fact that her house, the original of Green Knowe, is now in suburbia. The sea, she says, is still real and undiminished. Certainly the sea dominates *The Sea Egg*, as the house dominates the earlier books. Yet it is hard to think of the sea, even in literary terms, as a refuge. The associations are all the other way round. While a house is rooted, unmoving, reassuring, comfortable, safe, the sea is restless, perilous, inhospitable to creatures like ourselves who normally walk on land and breathe air. The sea is a challenge. In spite of Mrs Boston's own words, *The Sea Egg* seems to me to be a reaching out rather than a retreat. It demonstrates, incidentally, that the house is not so essential to her writing as was once thought.

The egg is a greenish stone which Toby and Jo, on holiday in Cornwall, put into a pool in a secluded cove. It hatches into a little triton, two-tailed, with dark blue eyes and hair 'like finest white crisp seaweed'. The triton grows up quickly. One night they hear his horn, go down to the sea, and are led to a watery cave where the seals gather with the triton as their leader. The boys swim with them. Next day their holiday ends; the season is over and the sea turbulent and threatening as autumn comes in:

> Now and again a particularly powerful wave would form itself with a long foaming head and muscle its way through the tumult with a tearing roar, throwing up stones ahead of it. The air re-echoed with toppling crashes, whip-cracks and the high rattle of shingle, over a continuous fiendish rumble.
>
> By noon there was a new development. Out to sea appeared a series of high ridges like the roof tops of whole Cornish streets, one behind the other. They came from the horizon moving steadily in threes, marbled but forming no crests until they were well up the slope of the cove. There

> they suddenly rose to a towering height, a crest sprang up with terrifying instantaneous ease, and they broke with a roll of thunder and a drumming that shook the shore.

There is something in *The Sea Egg* of the Boston themes of growth, of the finding of freedom, of learning through the senses. But the scale and movement of the story come from the sea, as seen in its many moods. The boys, their parents, the local folk, even the triton himself, are lightly sketched by comparison. In this book the power and beauty of Mrs Boston's style are fully matched by the power and beauty of what she is describing. For all the reputation of the Green Knowe books, I do not believe she has written anything finer than *The Sea Egg*.

L. M. Boston writes:

I was born in 1892, and even for that faraway date my parents were old-fashioned and so unlikely that I can hardly believe my memories are of real people. The family was rigidly, rabidly puritanical. Music, art, drama, dancing, and pleasure were all wicked. My mother thought even good food unnecessary to salvation, and therefore wrong. The most important parental influence over my life was by being specifically taught that I was born and bred to be a martyr, by burning at the stake; it was my destiny and my duty. This I have never felt up to, and have laboured all my life under a sense of absolute spiritual failure.

We lived in a featureless, new, uninspiring town full of wealth and churches, and my memories would show a starvation of everything but hymns and sermons, if we had not moved into the country for my mother's health. This was when I was eleven, and from that moment, life was as different as for a butterfly getting out of its chrysalis, became then like the children in my books: all eyes, ears, and finger tips in a world too beautiful to take in. Every moment of day and night was bliss, and had to be prolonged with solitary rambles in the early dawn, of which my elders had certainly no idea. There was no keeping me in, day or night, wet or fine. This, I suppose, is why my book-children are early rovers.

We lived in the north, and my sister and I were sent away to boarding school as far south as possible, to correct our north-country accent. We were, of course, great oddities and were unmercifully ragged and very unhappy. But we learnt to ride and had wild gallops on an old racecourse on the Downs. I went to a finishing school in Paris, thence to Oxford to read English, which I cut short for service in a French hospital in World War I. France became my country of adoption.

However, I married an English officer in the Flying Corps, as that romantic pioneering body was called. I have one son, the original Tolly—well qualified to draw his own dog, his own toys, his own toy box. I am not a traveller, but have wandered in France, Italy, Austria and Hungary, and studied painting in Vienna. I believe that one place closely explored will yield more than continents passed through.

Now I have found the place I need, and though postcards from abroad excite me to fever point, this is where I stay, getting deeper in it every moment and always surprised. This is the house that all the books describe. If I were a historian, a lifetime could be spent researching into it. But I just sit and talk to it. I live in it alone and find it good company.

And here are some extracts from a talk which Mrs Boston gave to the Children's Book Circle in November 1968:

Is there a conscious difference in the way I write for grown-ups and children? No, there is no difference of approach, style, vocabulary or standard. I could pick out passages from any of the books and you would not be able to tell what age it was aimed at. There is a difference in the range of experiences evoked . . .

Today the house is in suburbia . . . My darling Green Knowe has dwindled . . . There is not room for it to be. This may account for the flight to *The Sea Egg*. The sea is still real, undiminished. My approach has always been to explore reality as it appears, and from within to see how far imagination can properly expand it. Reality, after all, has no outside edge. I never start with a fantasy and look for a peg to hang it on. As far as I deliberately try to do anything other than to write a book that pleases me, I would like to remind adults of joy, now considered obsolete—and would like to encourage children to use and trust their senses for themselves at first hand—their ears, eyes and noses, their fingers and the soles of their feet, their skins and their breathing, their muscular joy and rhythms and heartbeats, their instinctive loves and pity and their awe of the unknown. This, not the telly, is the primary material of thought. It is from direct sense stimulus that imagination is born . . .

L. M. Boston

The Sea Egg is almost wholly an evocation of sense perception. The triton is so implicit in the sea-stuff that he hardly needed to be mentioned. He gets perhaps a dozen sentences to himself in the whole book – a mere flick of sea foam – but the sound of the sea is on every page.

L. M. Boston

Bibliography

Books for children:

THE CHILDREN OF GREEN KNOWE. Faber and Faber, 1954; Harcourt Brace, 1955.

THE CHIMNEYS OF GREEN KNOWE. Faber and Faber, 1958; Harcourt Brace, 1958, as THE TREASURE OF GREEN KNOWE.

THE RIVER AT GREEN KNOWE. Faber and Faber, 1959; Harcourt Brace, 1959.

A STRANGER AT GREEN KNOWE. Faber and Faber, 1961; Harcourt Brace, 1961.

AN ENEMY AT GREEN KNOWE. Faber and Faber, 1964; Harcourt Brace, 1964.

THE CASTLE OF YEW. The Bodley Head, 1965; Harcourt Brace, 1965.

THE SEA EGG. Faber and Faber, 1967; Harcourt Brace, 1967.

THE HOUSE THAT GREW. Faber and Faber, 1969.

THE HORNED MAN. (*A play.*) Faber and Faber, 1970.

NOTHING SAID. Faber and Faber, 1971; Harcourt Brace, 1971.

Short stories for children by L. M. Boston include *Curfew* in THE HOUSE OF THE NIGHTMARE AND OTHER EERIE TALES, edited by Kathleen Lines (The Bodley Head, 1967; Farrar, Straus and Giroux, 1968), and *Many Coloured Glass* in YOUNG WINTER'S TALES I, edited by M. R. Hodgkin (Macmillan, London, 1970).

H. F. Brinsmead

Hesba Fay Brinsmead was born in 1922 in the Blue Mountains of New South Wales, Australia. Before and after her marriage at the age of twenty, she held a variety of jobs, mostly connected with teaching and with the stage. Later she wrote stories, articles, and radio talks. Her first book, Pastures of the Blue Crane, *won the Mary Gilmore Medal (an Australian prize) and was chosen as best children's book of the year in Australia for 1964. It was followed by* Season of the Briar *(1965),* Beat of the City *(1966),* A Sapphire for September *(1967), and* Isle of the Sea Horse *(1969). She has two grown-up sons.*

Adolescents have always been around; teenagers only arrived a few years ago. The etymology indicates the difference between the two states. An adolescent is growing up; he is in transit between childhood and adult life. In my own boyhood, just before World War II, the conventional wisdom was that adolescence was a rather miserable time to be got through as painlessly as possible. It was assumed that the adolescent's chief aim in life was to become an adult. The teenager is a post-war phenomenon; he is not *becoming* something, he *is* something; and he may be as contemptuous of adult life as he is of childhood. Syd and Sabie, the teenage boys in H. F. Brinsmead's novel *Beat of the City*, comfort themselves at times when the grownups are being tiresome by recalling The Slogan: 'We are the only generation to be born superior to our parents.'

Mrs Brinsmead's novels are for teenagers and are mostly *about* teenagers. No pre-adolescent child has a significant part to play in any of them. The teenagers come and go, as teenagers will, in a crowd; they are always on the move. The books themselves are full of warmth and energy and tend to have large casts, plenty of incident, and unusual richness of background. Not only do things happen; people change and develop. All Mrs

Brinsmead's books are concerned with what she herself calls 'the problem of how to cope with life'. They are also concerned with the stage which comes before coping: namely finding out who and what you are.

She is particularly good at drawing the teenager *as* teenager. Adolescent characters in novels by other contemporary writers (for instance Gwyn, Roger and Alison in Alan Garner's *The Owl Service*; Christina, Mark and Will in K. M. Peyton's *Flambards*) are shown as the people they essentially are and always will be. It is not difficult to imagine them at the ages of 25, 35 or 45. But Mrs Brinsmead's Syd and Sabie in *Beat of the City*, and Binny in *A Sapphire for September*, are specifically sixteen-year-olds, and their age is part of their character. Last year they were not as they are now; next year they will be different again; their self-discovery is still going on, and in discovering themselves they are still changing. (The difference here between Mrs Brinsmead and the other writers mentioned is not a matter of superiority or inferiority on either side; it lies partly in style of characterization, partly in the kind of person created.) And Mrs Brinsmead has an interesting way of moving into and out of her characters' minds, of seeing them now from inside, now from outside, in a way that gives perspective to her portraits. Sometimes she manages, curiously, to be both inside and outside at once. This is Sabie, preserving a tactical silence while being ticked off by his father:

> In theory one does not quarrel with one's ever-loving parents. If they insist on admonishing and advising, one fills one's mind with a kind of inner, metallic music; this is a soporific and a panacea; it shuts out the world; it shuts out the future . . .
>
> A transistor with an earplug is good. It makes the perfect anaesthetic. But even without the transistor one can keep the confused metallic theme in one's mind. If one stands and stares with one's mouth hanging open and a certain blank expression on one's face—vacant, yet studied—listening as it were to the beat jazz-time of one's own pulse—and occasionally, with a quiet, maddening rhythm, clicking one's fingers at one's sides—why then, from the parent, or parents, one gets a reaction.

Right now his father was saying, 'But don't you have any ambition, boy? Don't you want to succeed?'

Well, not saying. Yelling, to put it bluntly.

Here the reader 'is' Sabie, but at the same time is seeing him from the viewpoint of an irritated parent. If a generation gap exists – and in Mrs Brinsmead's books it exists in individual cases such as this, not as a general phenomenon – the author is on both sides of it.

A combination of sympathy and detachment in her treatment of teenagers is indeed one of Mrs Brinsmead's strengths. It is already apparent in her first book, *Pastures of the Blue Crane*, which was published in 1964. This is the story of Ryl, a poor little fairly-rich girl who cares for nobody but whose cramped character unwinds when she finds herself joint owner of a run-down farm with her proletarian grandfather Dusty. Self-centred, stoical, snobby Ryl is one of those rare, infuriating heroines whom one doesn't much like but finds oneself caring about – presumably because the author, while seeing her clearly for the rather unlovable person she is, can also feel with her and perceive what she might become.

The four-dimensional character study of Ryl, over a period in which she changes greatly yet remains recognizably the same girl, is as fine in its way as anything Mrs Brinsmead has done. She has not again penetrated any individual to the same depth. Many of her young people are appealing, especially the girls: Gisela, the small person with the big voice and big boots in *Season of the Briar*; the cheerful urchin Binny in *A Sapphire for September*; sensitive Emma in *Isle of the Sea Horse*. But they are more lightly sketched than Ryl, and the reader does not become involved with them in the same way. This is probably because of a tendency to put a group, rather than a single individual, at the centre of a story. Gisela, Binny and Emma can be considered as the heroines of the books in which they appear, but they do not dominate the scene.

Beat of the City, Mrs Brinsmead's 'biggest' book so far, has four young people at its heart: two boys and two girls. But this is not only a book about what happens to certain individuals; it is also a portrayal of a city and a composite study of the life of young people in it; it is an exploration, too, of certain values and relationships. It is a bold and forceful novel and, taken as a whole, is Mrs Brinsmead's most impressive book up to the time of writing. Where many authors have found it easier to concentrate on the enduring realities of human nature if they avoid those immediate surface details which are so hard to get right and so sure to fall out of date, *Beat of the City* is uncompromisingly contemporary. 'In Melbourne in 1965 the way-outs were in', it begins; and the Melbourne of 1965—no other time, no other place—is the setting of this story. And, paradoxically but deservedly, the sense of immediacy has so far proved lasting, for although it is no longer 1965 the feeling that everything is happening here and now remains fresh and strong.

The plot of *Beat of the City* is worked out in intricate detail; the characters are carefully balanced. Sabie's parents are well-to-do upper-middle-class; Syd's are plebeian. Mary lives with her uncle, a pastor. Raylene is a motherless urchin, drawn to the bright lights as moth to candle. The four lives come together, interact, tangle with danger and delinquency; and after some alarming incidents, including a near-rape, they disentangle, with Sabie and Raylene, the more mixed-up of the kids, well on the way to unmixing themselves.

Each character in turn moves into and out of the spotlight; but in spite of the lack of a continuous focus the story does not fall apart. What holds it together is the most impressive element of all, the city of Melbourne itself. Melbourne is alive on every page, beginning with the first:

> On the West Bank there is the jam-packed, claptrap, shindig-filled old inner suburb of Abbotsford, running into Fitzroy and Carlton so that nobody knows where one ends and the other begins, a hugger-mugger of factories, tenements, migrant hostels and almost brand-new slums bursting with folk coming in all colours, shapes and sizes. Half submerged by it on the one side but with the quiet of the river at its shoulders is the ivory tower, the stone-turreted Convent where the soft-spoken Sisters live, and wait upon the poor. The city batters and rattles at their gates, but behind them are their incongruous water meadows, and

> the river. The gardener, Manuel, and rosy Sister Martha of the Beatitudes are picking sweetcorn from the vegetable garden. Two hundred yards from the swish of traffic over the Big Bridge the Sisters' cows come sedately over the bridle-path on their way home to be milked.

The theme of the novel is the pursuit of happiness, as carried out by various people in various ways through the streets, homes and haunts of the city. Sabie's mother, expressing what it is safe to assume are the author's own views, contrasts true happiness—something to be built from your own inner resources—with an instant, ready-mixed substitute symbolized by the Tootle Bird, a mythical creature that 'probably nests in a box of empty Coke bottles' and has a call like the whirring noise of a fruit machine. This direct expression of view comes in a natural way at an appropriate moment, and does no harm to the story; but it is a pointer, I think, to the book's major flaw. One has a persistent sense that the characters and action have been designed to illustrate this very message.

The clash of values is direct and simple. Sabie and Raylene both look for 'kicks', and both come close to disaster. Mary and, increasingly, Syd create their own pleasures and are sensible and constructive. The good girl Mary, whose approach to life is the opposite of that summed up in the quest for the Tootle Bird, seems to me to be altogether too good to be true. Pains are taken to indicate that her activities, such as folk-singing, dancing and playing the clarinet, are livelier and more with-it than canned amusements; yet the result is only to make her less convincing, less likeable. Like all excessively good fictional characters, she becomes a shade tiresome.

Emergence of the author's values is not in itself objectionable. In a story with a contemporary setting where the subject-matter, broadly, is what life is about, suppression would be difficult and in any case not praiseworthy. The point at which damage starts is when character or action is distorted, or the impression given that the story is only a vehicle for carrying a message. In *Beat of the City* the action, even if contrived, is strong, and the characters, except perhaps Mary, come alive as people. The damage is slight and the book can stand it. And it is possible that the author's strength of feeling about true and false happiness has provided the book's motive force, and is responsible for its power as well as its weakness.

Of Mrs Brinsmead's first five novels, the remaining three are slighter than *Beat of the City* or *Pastures of the Blue Crane*. Her second book, *Season of the Briar*, is an episodic story about four young men who form a weed-spraying unit in Tasmania; about their encounters with a party of trampers and with a tiny remote community, during which they make some discoveries about themselves and each other. In *A Sapphire for September* Binny, slightly common but full of fizz and goodwill, joins a club of gem-seekers with her eye on handsome but elusive student Adam; she doesn't get him, but at the end can pick herself up and dust herself down, a bit older, a bit wiser. Emma, in *Isle of the Sea Horse*, is cast away on a pleasant-enough desert island with a group of people who, like herself, are in no hurry to go back to mainland life; but they have to face it in the end. These books are still concerned with 'the problem of how to cope with life', but they are less closely at grips and their situations are more specialized.

Mrs Brinsmead is a writer with several faults. The structure of her stories can be unsatisfactory: notably in *Pastures of the Blue Crane*, which falls away in the second half, and *Season of the Briar*, which lacks any clear focal point and never really pulls itself together at all. Her male characters are rarely memorable. She is apt to scatter minor figures around without taking enough pains to make them live for the reader, although it is plain that they live for *her*, and she even has an endearing habit in her novels of throwing parties for them. What is so attractive about her is her writing personality. There is a sense of the author's presence, of her sympathy with the people she is writing for and about. Her settings have ranged widely and are strongly realized. Her vitality compensates for a great many failings. The last thing one would wish on her, the negation of her true gift, would be a cool perfection.

H. F. Brinsmead writes:

I took my primary school classes by correspondence, as our village was remote indeed in those days. My father had a sawmill, my mother was a professional bulb-grower. At that time our nearest neighbour was three miles away, the road little more than a track made by my father's bullock team, and the nearest railhead was Richmond, thirty miles away. Later my father took on the local mail run—this was when a post office was opened at Bilpin, a mere six miles away. Previously my father and mother had been in the mission field in Java—my father was clever at languages and interpreted and translated Dutch, Chinese and Javanese into English. My mother was of good old Cockney stock; my father's people came from Wiltshire.

I was the youngest of five children—four girls and a boy. Later on, I went to a church school at Wahroonga, a Sydney suburb, and did part of a teacher's training course; but I hated it, left college, and went to the Western sheep country, and then to the Derwent Valley in Tasmania, as a governess. I also had stage and voice training, with a view to being a radio announcer, but at the ripe old age of twenty got married instead. I had always written poetry, and said that I wanted to be a writer, but in those times it was almost a dirty word, and I was always told to put such thoughts from me and learn some useful thing, like cooking.

After marriage, while the two boys were small, I had various jobs: an interesting, though sad, one was teaching a little deaf girl to speak while she still had some slight hearing, before it should go entirely. This was one of the most rewarding things I have ever done. I also was a 'supervisor' in a kindergarten, and at one time was endeavouring to control sixty small children, all on my own. Then, going back to the idea of stage or radio, I joined a repertory group. But after a long time I woke up to the fact that this world was not the one for me. I have always valued freedom very highly, and it seemed—still does—that acting people are all sorts of prisoners, locked in by fear of producers, the public, their rivals, their image . . .

When well into my thirties, I managed to scrape together the fees to take a correspondence course in journalism. Quite soon I found that editors would buy my stories and articles. I did a lot of talks for the Australian Broadcasting Corporation. Probably the best thing that ever happened to me was when the ABC told me that they had been using too many of my talks when I was only a freelance and not on the staff, and that I should not send them any more for six months. Then I had to look for another market and began to write a book, *Pastures of the Blue Crane*. I have been doing it ever since.

As a writer I am a loner at heart, a solitary. But am I ever alone? Right now, I'm looking after a household of six souls—with prospects of another four, just visitors for a few weeks during the school holidays—and this is typical. Some time each year, in order to get anywhere, I have to hire a caravan, in a caravan park a mile or so from my home, to work in.

I began writing for teenagers because at the time my own children were that, and also many nephews and nieces, and they fascinated me. They still do. I don't know that I have a lot to say to adults. There are already too many people talking at once, saying the same things. I might do an adult novel some time, but not at the expense of leaving a teenage story unwritten. The young ones are the relevant people today. They are far too much exploited: I'm sure it is the greedy, grasping oldies who chivvy them into drug-taking, pill-taking, weird clothes and all the other crimes laid at their door. I like to think that my books, in their small way, peddle a commodity that's getting rarer all the time—the thing called hope. All my themes probably concern the problem of how to cope with life. It's no use writing books about that for us oldies; we've already lost the glorious fight, and cheerfully, too.

H. F. Brinsmead

Bibliography

PASTURES OF THE BLUE CRANE. Oxford University Press, 1964; Coward-McCann, 1966.

SEASON OF THE BRIAR. Oxford University Press, 1965; Coward-McCann 1967.

BEAT OF THE CITY. Oxford University Press, 1966; Coward-McCann, 1967.

A SAPPHIRE FOR SEPTEMBER. Oxford University Press, 1967; Coward-McCann, 1968.

ISLE OF THE SEA HORSE. Oxford University Press, 1969.

LISTEN TO THE WIND. Oxford University Press, 1970.

A short story, *The Twilight Road*, was published in MISCELLANY FOUR, edited by Edward Blishen (Oxford University Press, 1967).

John Christopher

*John Christopher was born in Knowsley, Lancashire, in 1922. His family moved south to Hampshire when he was ten, and he was educated at Peter Symonds' School, Winchester. After demobilization from the Army he spent two years as a freelance writer with the help of a grant from the Rockefeller Foundation, and then worked until 1958 in an information bureau of the Diamond Corporation. Since 1958 he has been a full-time professional writer. He is married, with a son and four daughters, and lives in Guernsey, in the Channel Islands. His books for children include the 'Tripods' trilogy—*The White Mountains *(1967),* The City of Gold and Lead *(1967), and* The Pool of Fire *(1968)—and* The Lotus Caves *(1969).*

The traditional adventure story for boys, coming down to us from such writers as Stevenson, Ballantyne and Henty, is in sorry decline today. The far horizons have shrunk. The printed word cannot compete with film or television in presenting straightforward action; and, in any case, the made-up adventure story is frequently outshone by real-life achievements, brought instantly home to us by the electronic media.

In this context, the opportunities for science fiction seem obvious. It can re-expand our diminished world, can give the writer a chance of outpacing hard fact and exploring any number of rich and strange hypotheses. What is more, it allows him to examine nature in an infinite variety of contexts.

In Britain at least, science fiction for children has been disappointing. By and large, the best children's writers have not felt impelled towards science fiction, while the best science fiction writers have not felt impelled to write for children. John Christopher is an exception. He is an established novelist who had already mastered his craft when he came to children's books, and who has put his full talent into them.

John Christopher

He is a prolific writer, with something like forty books to his credit altogether. He has written 'serious' adult novels under his own name (which is not John Christopher); and, under other names, books which include light comedy, detective thrillers, and even two with cricket backgrounds. The Christopher novels for adults, he says, though commonly described as science fiction, 'are in fact adventure stories involving a study of human reactions to severe environmental stresses'. This would also be a fair description of his first five books for children, the 'Tripods' trilogy, *The Lotus Caves* and *The Guardians*.

John Christopher's work makes more sense than most out of that elusive border between children's and adult fiction. Adult novels such as *The Death of Grass* (1956), *A Wrinkle in the Skin* (1965) and *Pendulum* (1968) postulate catastrophes of various kinds, just as the 'Tripods' trilogy does for children. All show people struggling to survive and make a comeback. The adult novels contain a good dcal of scx and violcncc: not automatically 'unsuitable' for children, who are well enough aware that sex and violence exist, but here handled in a way that requires an adult understanding and frame of reference. Sex is not simply a matter of the sexual act; it is a force working on people in obscure and powerful ways. Violence in these novels is no mere 'bang-you're-dead' matter; it can be disturbingly brutal and casual, or the outcome of complicated social and psychological processes.

Like many writers of, or on the borders of, science fiction, John Christopher is much concerned with man and society, and here again his adult novels demand a kind of awareness, a kind of understanding that are reached in maturity if at all. The children's books do not assume less intelligence in the reader, but they do and must assume less knowledge and experience of the world. And yet they are just as serious as the adult books; and they seem to me to be better written. The 'Tripods' trilogy and *The Lotus Caves* show John Christopher at his best, both in construction of story and in his handling of the English language, which is such as to give positive aesthetic pleasure to an adult reader.

The theme of the trilogy is the struggle of a few remaining free men against the Masters. The Masters are superior beings who have come from a distant world and are ruling this one through the Tripods: gleaming metal hemispheres on three articulated legs, several times as high as a church. The Masters look on people rather as we look on animals, and tame them by a form of mental castration called 'capping', carried out in adolescence. The earth's technology has been destroyed, and people live in a plodding, neo-medieval peace. The defeat of the formidable Masters by a few men who have escaped capping might seem a wild improbability; but the Masters are vulnerable in two ways. One is that they are surviving by artificial means in an inhospitable environment; they cannot breathe the air and have to live in three domed cities of their own with a special atmosphere. The other is that they assume men to be fully under control and a rebellion to be impossible.

In the first book, *The White Mountains* (1967), the hero, Will Parker, runs away from being capped and travels with two friends to join the rebel band in its mountain refuge. In *The City of Gold and Lead* (1967), Will and another boy gain admission as slaves to the Masters' city. With the aid of what they learn, the rebels are able to destroy the city in the third book, *The Pool of Fire* (1968). The story forms a true trilogy; it is not just one novel cut into three slices. The books are self-contained, yet each is part of a logical larger whole, and each has its own climax, with the third book providing in the destruction of the Masters' city the climax to the whole story. Unfortunately, in the latter part of *The Pool of Fire*, this climax is followed by a double anticlimax: a campaign against another of the Masters' cities, and then a wrangle among men when it is all over. To destroy one city would surely have been enough for the story; and the wrangling, though sadly probable, is not very exciting or dramatic.

One problem which is not solved, and perhaps in its nature is insoluble, is that of giving the Masters a convincing appearance. Invented forms of life are apt to be either totally unimaginable or else grotesque. The Masters are walking, three-legged, treelike creatures. I am not too surprised that the artist does not venture to portray one on a jacket. Yet the trilogy is a fine achievement: its most haunting moment perhaps being when the three boys discover a great city of the Ancients—that is, ourselves—lying open and abandoned, under a perpetual tabu of the capped.

John Christopher's fourth book for children, *The Lotus Caves* (1969), is set on the moon at a future time when it is no longer an exciting place. Under a structure called the Bubble is a fifty-year-old research station, staffed by people on long contracts without home leave. The taxpayers back home foot the bill and are not inclined to pay for many luxuries. Marty is a boy who gets bored and sets off on an unofficial excursion outside the Bubble in a 'crawler', with his non-conforming friend Steve. And they fall by accident into a cavern: one of a linked series where they find air and water, taste and colour, light and sound and movement, a richness unknown on the moon's bleak surface.

This is the realm of the Plant: vast, intelligent, self-absorbed, and beneficent – but for reasons of self-preservation disinclined to let anyone go back and tell the tale. One man has entered the caves before the boys: he is Thurgood, who happily worships the Plant, lives on its delicious fruit, and grows no older. Marty and Steve will become like him unless they get away before being totally captivated. So, in the 'night' which comes when the Plant withdraws into meditation and switches off its awareness of all that goes on, they plan their escape . . .

There are elements here of Arcadia, of Eden, of Shangri-La, as well as of the Odyssey, from which the title and theme in part are drawn. It is a strange and memorable story, perhaps as much fantasy as science fiction, yet raising issues which are easily translated into practical terms. A demanding benevolence is by no means unknown in human relationships. On a second reading one notes what could easily be missed the first time round – a subtle change in the relationship between the two boys. Steve is the loner, the odd-boy-out, but it is Marty who can better resist the Plant and who assumes the leadership. The author has avoided the too-easy assumption that the non-conformist has necessarily more inner strength.

The Guardians (1970) is concerned with the British class system projected into the future and polarized. We are eighty years on, and the 'two nations' have split completely. There is now on the one hand the Conurb, where the masses live – a place of processed food, pop song, mindless entertainment, mechanized sport which generates occasional partisan violence as a safety valve. And on the other side of a high fence, cut off from the Conurb psychologically as well as physically, is the County, where the gentry have successfully put the clock back and lead a leisured rural life in well-staffed country houses, engaging in time-honoured country pursuits. (Interestingly, neither Conurbans nor gentry have any use for books.) The Guardians are the small group who keep both parts of this neatly divided society under control. As prophecy this would be the longest of long shots: whichever way we are going, we do not seem likely to arrive at that particular state of affairs. But, of course, it is not prophecy; it is hypothesis or, more exactly, extrapolation, for here are opposing value-systems developed to the ultimate degree.

The hero Rob is a loner, out of place in the conditioned society of the Conurb, who crosses the Fence and finds a place for himself as the supposed long-lost cousin of a County family. And as Rob becomes assimilated into the gentry, the upper-class boy Mike, who helped this ragged Conurban boy and found him to be human, develops seditious tendencies and becomes involved in a revolutionary movement. Although *The Guardians*, like its predecessors, can be read as a story of action and of human interest, its socio-political framework is more obtrusive, perhaps to the point of damaging it as a novel.

The common thread of all the five novels is a preoccupation with the question of freedom and authority: painful freedom and comfortable submission to authority. While the author (like Aldous Huxley in *Brave New World* and George Orwell in *1984*) is clearly on the side of freedom, he never presents it as an unthought-about, self-evident good. Sharp and disconcerting, the thought recurs – most notably at the end of *The Lotus Caves* – that the acceptance of authority can, in some ways, be enviable. The case for freedom is not that freedom is nice, but that it demands more from us – demands the qualities that make us human. John Christopher is at grips with a fundamental question, and this gives weight to his novels; his own talents give them distinction.

He is also a highly professional writer with a proper willingness to produce an exciting story and keep it moving along. In one minor way he seems to have followed a convention of the old adventure stories for boys: the five books discussed have, to all intents and purposes, no girls in them. This seems to derive from the accepted view that girls will read boys' books but boys will not read books for girls. Yet John Christopher's adult novels make it clear that he is perfectly well able to create feminine characters, and it is possible that the exclusion will not continue.

John Christopher has this to say about his books for children:

I had been a writer for nearly twenty years, a full-time professional novelist for eight, before I made any real attempt to write for children. Hamish Hamilton approached my London agent and asked if they could commission me to write a science-fiction story for boys. I do not approve of commissions and refused, but a few months later wrote the book anyway.

A copy went to my American agent and was shown to Macmillan in the United States. They thought the book started well but then fell apart; in fact it needed a complete rewriting. I am very bad at revision and my first impulse was to refuse: the book had been accepted by Hamilton as it stood and there was a fair chance that it might be taken by some other American publisher. When I came to study Macmillan's detailed criticisms, however, I could not deny their validity. I realized they were quite right – the book after the opening chapters did fall apart.

I was forced to realize something else as well – that this almost certainly derived from my having tackled the book with the feeling, subconscious possibly but no less important for that, that it was 'only a juvenile'. One did not need to give it such concentrated attention as one would an adult novel. Once I saw this I accepted the reproof and the redirection. I wrote the book again, part of it a third time. This final version was preferred by both publishers. While a poor judge (as probably most writers are) of my own work, even I could see that it was overwhelmingly superior to the first draft.

This was *The White Mountains*. With the second book I only had the first chapter to rewrite and the third was accepted as it stood. Any illusions I might have had about mastering my craft were shattered when my fourth book, *The Lotus Caves*, was found as far wanting as the first had been. Once again complete rewriting was called for, and the same happened with the fifth book, *The Guardians*.

There are writers who enjoy working with editors on their books; who, for that matter, enjoy revising. I have been told of one distinguished writer for children who almost had to have the manuscript torn from him to go to the printer after years of reworking. I respect and envy him but I still hate it. Fortunately I am blessed with editors, in London and New York, who apart from having unerring eyes for the false step are both kind and tactful. If I ever do succeed in getting things right, I will owe a very great deal to them.

What I have learned is that writing for children is at least as exacting and concentration-demanding as writing for adults. But one can add another word: stimulating. It is the form of writing which I can now least imagine giving up.

John Christopher

Bibliography

Novels for children:

THE WHITE MOUNTAINS. Hamish Hamilton, 1967; Macmillan, 1967.
THE CITY OF GOLD AND LEAD. Hamish Hamilton, 1967; Macmillan, 1967.
THE POOL OF FIRE. Hamish Hamilton, 1968; Macmillan, 1968.
THE LOTUS CAVES. Hamish Hamilton, 1969; Macmillan, 1969.
THE GUARDIANS. Hamish Hamilton, 1970; Macmillan, 1970.
THE PRINCE IN WAITING. Hamish Hamilton, 1970; Macmillan, 1970.
BEYOND THE BURNING LANDS. Hamish Hamilton, 1971; Macmillan, 1971

Helen Cresswell

Helen Cresswell was born in Nottingham, the middle child of three. She went to Nottingham Girls' High School and King's College, London, where she took an honours degree in English. She has worked for the BBC and has taught children of various ages. She is in her early thirties, is married (to Brian Rowe) and has a daughter called Caroline. She lives in the country near Nottingham. Her books for children include The Piemakers *(1967)*, The Signposters *(1968), and* The Night-Watchmen *(1969).*

Helen Cresswell is a young and prolific writer who, beginning in 1960, produced at least twenty books in her first ten years as a published author. There is nothing wrong with being prolific. Some writers are, some are not. Probably there is no relationship, either direct or inverse, between productivity and literary merit. But there seems to be a limit to the number of books of distinction that one person can write over a given period; and prolific authors generally turn out a proportion of secondary work. Miss Cresswell has written several books that are slight, and some that are inferior. But her best is very good, and her slighter books have often shown true quality.

There are two main strands in her work: poetic fantasy and humour. The gift for fantasy was there from the beginning, but has strengthened and deepened in later books. The humour, often hackneyed and obvious at first, has developed even more strikingly into the comic richness which accompanied the fantasy of *The Piemakers* (1967) and *The Night-Watchmen* (1969).

Where fantasy and humour lay side by side in an early book, the fantasy was clearly of a different quality from the humour. The difference can be seen in *The White Sea Horse* (1964): the story of the small, magical horse that Molly's fisherman father found in his nets. Here is the account of how Molly first saw it:

> In the Tubby Boat there was a hot hungry smell of stew, the light from the fire stroked the walls and the shadows yawned and stretched like sleepy cats. Molly's father laid the animal on the patchwork rug before the fire. Molly knelt beside it, staring in wonder.
>
> It was a tiny horse of purest white, so delicate that he seemed to be carved from ice. His hooves were of gold and they shone yellow in the firelight, and his ears pricked like petals, as though he were listening. His eyes were clear and yellow as September moons.

There is an equally excellent description of how Molly and her friend Peter look down from a boat through the green glassy depths of an enchanted sea. But the book is marred by the crudity of its comic element, involving the stock figure of the pompous Mayor, Mr Winkle:

> Mr Winkle stamped through the square and everyone stood aside in silence to let him pass. They could see that he was very angry. Just as he reached the bottom of the steps he slipped on a broken egg and sat promptly on the pavement. The people tittered and then tried to turn their titters into coughs, and Mr Winkle got up with as much dignity as possible. His face was like thunder.
>
> 'This is the most outrageous thing I have ever seen in my whole life,' he said. 'Those donkeys have deliberately chewed the heads off every single flower in my garden. They have stolen my hat and ruined the market . . . My mind is made up. The donkeys must go. By seven o'clock to-morrow morning there must not be a single donkey left in Piskerton, or – or –'
>
> He choked hard and tried to think of something to say. 'Or else!' he said at last.

Mr Winkle could come from any of a thousand third-rate stories. He is not in the same imaginative world as the improbable tramp Josh, with the wild grey tufts of eyebrows and the voice 'rich and with built-in echoes as if it were in church', who suddenly appears in *The Night-Watchmen* five years later:

> Sun struck the dew that glinted on his hair and beard.

Wild, wicked and impossible he loomed among the clipped, self-respecting laurels.

Stock figures on the level of Mr Winkle also populate the 'Jumbo' books, of which the first, *Jumbo Spencer*, was published in 1963, and which were the main channel for Helen Cresswell's humour at that time. These were strongly reminiscent of Richmal Crompton's 'William' books. Jumbo, like William, is a small boy who is the unquestioned leader of his gang of four, imaginative in a naive way, forever organizing clubs and exhibitions and absurdly ambitious projects. Unlike William, Jumbo also impresses the adult population with his abilities, and can call meetings which the whole of his village attends. He is successful on a big scale, starring in TV programmes, putting the village on the map, establishing legends, starting a dig that leads to real Anglo-Saxon treasures, getting a village hall built. He represents the wildest wish-fulfilment of the small boy as a member of his society. I find him, like William, engaging; but I would never have expected the creator of Jumbo to be also the creator of *The Piemakers*.

This was the book with which Miss Cresswell came into her own. It has all the qualities which should enable a children's book to last. The story it tells is memorable, funny, and unlike any other; it is dateless – being set in the past indefinite of rural England – and it has an equal appeal to child and adult, so that grown-ups can remember it with pleasure and share it with their own children and the child within. For adults there is the bonus of seeing more than the child can be expected to do: the accuracy of the family relationships, the mock-heroic nature of the whole story.

It is about the Rollers of Danby Dale – Arthy, Jem and Gravella – and the enormous pie they bake when the King, 'being desirous of supping on a pie of the Dales', offers a prize of 100 guineas and the honour of royal appointment to 'the Piemaker of the Dales who shall by the third day of June make a pie the biggest and best by common consent'. Backed by the people of Danby Dale, Arthy bakes a pie for two thousand: the biggest pie in the history of the world, involving strict security precautions and the manufacture by the blacksmith at Wedbury of a pie-dish so huge that it has to be floated down the river like a boat.

A pie of epic grandeur is a comic paradox in itself, and the author has developed it to the utmost. We are told how a squad of strong men laid the crust over the top; after which Arthy and his helper

> began the last stage of that prodigious making. Gently the two men slid the sheet of metal under that exquisite centre-piece [the royal arms in pastry] so that not a curl, not a flourish was disturbed. And as carefully they carried it to the dish and set it at last in the middle of that wide white crust, the crowning perfection. As Arthy climbed down, a soft perceptible sigh ran through the shadowy barn and all the toil of the day gathered into this one moment of achievement. The pie was ready for the oven.

Earlier we have heard how the crew which brought the pie-dish down the river stood watching it 'as it lay rocking gently at its moorings. The reddish gleam of the setting sun lit the polished metal to splendour, and Gravella thought there could never have been a more noble vessel.' And finally there is Arthy's triumph:

> Delicately the King's eyebrows arched and the doors of the barn opened slowly on great groaning hinges. There was sudden silence. Out from the shadows came the huge pie-dish, wheeled by twenty men with straining shoulders. The sun fell for the first time on to that glorious crust, perfectly smooth and brown, gleaming faintly. It was impossible, a miracle under that blue sky, standing among the grass and clover like some enormous fruit . . . For a full minute the pie stood there and more than three thousand people stood and stared in silence, made into statues by their disbelief. Then the roar that broke out sent the skylarks somersaulting skyward and the din broke in deafening fragments and Arthy was borne up into the air and shouldered to the King.

In this moment of wide-eyed wonder, humour and fantasy blend. The piemakers' achievement is absurd but it is marvellous; and the author is perfectly, properly, almost poetically serious about it.

Helen Cresswell

Among the ingredients of *The Piemakers* is nostalgia: a gentle, pleasing nostalgia for an innocent age of rural craftsmanship that probably never was. This nostalgia has increased in subsequent fantasies, and along with it has gone a preoccupation with the figure of the wandering artist whose freedom is threatened by an unsympathetic society. Only occasionally has there been the same sense of sheer delight. One hesitates to suggest, on slight evidence over a fairly short period, that it is a case of cause and effect, but it is possible to feel that the author has indulged her nostalgia too much and allowed this particular preoccupation to go too far. Certainly the three major books which up to the time of writing have followed *The Piemakers* have been less successful.

The Signposters (1968) is set in an England small and white and clean, an England of blue remembered hills, an England suspiciously close to being Merrie. Dyke Signposter's job of pacing out distances and painting signs allows him to be both artist and wanderer; his wife Hetty and daughter Barley go with him in the wagon drawn by the dawdling horse Cornish from Whipple to Plumtree, Plumtree to Makewith, Makewith to Haze. Complications arising from Dyke's ambition to bring about a great family reunion fill the long summer days of the story. The book is unfortunately placed in Helen Cresswell's work. Coming before *The Piemakers* it would have seemed to lead up to it; coming afterwards it is a slight disappointment, because it does a similar thing, and does it, though pleasantly enough, without quite the same joyous humour. *The Piemakers* is indeed the kind of book that an author cannot fruitfully aim to repeat, because it goes right to the end of its line; after it, the way ahead must be to do something different.

The Signposters and its successors *The Night-Watchmen* (1969) and *The Outlanders* (1970) seem increasingly to be expressing an attitude to life: a belief that spontaneity, individualism, creative artistry or craftsmanship, a readiness to move on and to take what life offers are virtues to be prized; rigidity and stuffiness are sins against the human spirit. The one unlikeable character in *The Signposters* is Uncle Wick, the candlemaker, whose candles 'were every one the same, except that some were short and fat and dull and others were long and thin and dull'; and even

Uncle Wick comes good in the end and starts making his candles curled and coloured and all different.

The Night-Watchmen has a darker streak. Two tramps Josh and Caleb, who are comic eccentrics but are also artist-wanderers – for Josh is a would-be writer and Caleb an imaginative cook – are driven by the jealous Greeneyes from their camp beside a hole in the road; and it appears that this is continually happening to them. Is, then, the freedom of the artist a fugitive thing: is he always to be the victim of jealous pursuit? The author has said that she did not know the Greeneyes were going to move in, and that she would have put up a fight against them if she had realized what a misery they were going to be. She has also said that 'you don't choose symbols – they choose you'. *The Night-Watchmen* is something of a mystery, for the story is told from over the shoulder of a boy who is convalescing from illness, and at the end he is not sure whether Josh and Caleb and the Greeneyes ever existed; but whether it all 'really' happened or whether it is an externalization of something in the boy's mind does not greatly affect the issue. The implications are pessimistic; art and imagination are defeated.

In *The Outlanders* we are back in the indefinite past; the theme is the traditional one of the Quest. The Rhymers – a family threesome like the Piemakers and the Signposters – set out from the lumpish town of Bray in search of a Boy of unearthly radiance who has briefly stayed with them and who, they know, can grant their dearest wish. This quest is successful; *The Outlanders* is a more positive, a more hopeful book than *The Night-Watchmen*. But *The Night-Watchmen* seems to me more interesting; it seeks to combine comedy and fantasy in a way quite different from that of *The Piemakers*. The two tramps are rich, larger-than-life characters, encountered in what at least appears to be the here-and-now; the Greeneyes are a menacing intrusion from a fantasy world which is elsewhere. Comedy shot through with dark fantasy: I cannot readily think of anything *like* this in children's literature. Yet the book cannot be called satisfactory; too much is vague or flimsy or unresolved; one feels that the author has not grappled hard enough with her material. *The Outlanders* has an occasional dreamlike beauty of its own, but to my mind lacks substance; the blood is drained out of it by a numinous mysticism and a feeling that the whole story is allegorical and nothing is really happening at all.

It is difficult to say where Helen Cresswell is going at present. Her progress has been hit-and-miss; her best book, *The Piemakers*, came almost unpredictably out of the blue. She is clearly capable of doing something just as unpredictable and successful at any time. Possibly the prolific writer is in greater need of self-discipline than others whose progress is more painful, and occasionally I suspect that Miss Cresswell's facility has been her undoing and she has been satisfied too easily with her work. But she is a young writer with a strong creative flow who can afford to make a few false moves. These are early days in her career. Her development will be clearer in five or ten years' time; and it may well be impressive.

Helen Cresswell writes:

I rarely set out with any definite statement to make, and am usually well into a fantasy before I begin myself to see what it is saying. Carefully worked-out symbolism is almost always cliché. You don't choose symbols – they choose you. I'm a great believer in letting things happen as far as possible. This sounds very woolly and undisciplined but is in fact quite difficult, and needs a particular, very delicate balance between the workings of the conscious and unconscious minds. If I tried to work out a fantasy in advance with all the symbolism neatly tied up, it would be stone dead before I even started. In fact, I doubt whether I could be bothered to write it, because it would not be an exploration, and there would be nothing in it for me (or for anybody).

All the same, these fantasies do have meanings, they have meanings to begin with and they take on meanings of their own as they progress. If a fantasy *didn't* have a meaning, then there would be no point in publishing it – I mean, one person's fantasy is as good as another's, isn't it?

My own favourite book is still *The Piemakers*, partly because I think it the most nearly perfect in form (not that it's anywhere near enough) and partly because it marked a turning-point in my writing, and was the first book in which humour and fantasy became fused. Up till then, the humour had gone into the Jumbo books and the fantasy was unleavened with comedy. With *The Piemakers* I suddenly became conscious that I had found my 'voice' if this is not to use too high-flown a term. I also had more pleasure in the actual writing of this book than in any other before or since. I loved it, and still do.

As to why I write for children, I have no idea. I think it may partly be because primarily I have always thought of myself as a poet, having written poetry from childhood in enormous quantities, and I think that fantasy is in many ways an extension of poetry. Also, growing older is very often a growing into rigidity, and there is enormous fluidity and freedom of range possible in children's writing which would not be possible in any other form. Also, it is fun. Also, I have a very great respect for childhood, and like to be talking to human beings before they have become capable of pose or hypocrisy or prejudice. I think this is why my writing is for younger children, for real childhood. Also, I have always had a deep-rooted sense of what I can only describe as 'infinite possibility', a sort of glorious feeling of the unpredictability of things and their unlimited variety (a bit like what Gerard Manley Hopkins is talking about in his poem 'Pied Beauty') and this excites me very much, and keeps me going.

I probably seem too prolific to some people, but this I cannot help. I started writing a lot too early in life to be able to break the habit now. The passion for words has been the strongest and longest-lasting in my life so far, and I see no possibility of my ever being free from it. With it, equally deep-rooted (and I confess this at the risk of being thought hopelessly out of date) goes a passion for natural beauty and the English countryside, so that the two are almost inseparable. The temptation to launch into descriptive passages is sometimes almost irresistible, but in many ways writing for children has been good discipline, in that it has forced me to find the single evocative word or phrase where I might quite happily have written several paragraphs. I am very conscious of the 'spirit of place' and practically all my books are germinated by this feeling rather than by character, plot, message or anything else.

Helen Cresswell

Bibliography

SONYA-BY-THE-SHORE. Dent, 1960.

JUMBO SPENCER. Brockhampton Press, 1963; Lippincott, 1966.

THE WHITE SEA HORSE. Chatto, Boyd and Oliver, 1964; Lippincott, 1965.

JUMBO BACK TO NATURE. Brockhampton Press, 1965.

PIETRO AND THE MULE. Chatto, Boyd and Oliver, 1965; Bobbs-Merrill, 1970.

JUMBO AFLOAT. Brockhampton Press, 1966.

WHERE THE WIND BLOWS. Faber and Faber, 1966; Funk and Wagnalls, 1968.

A DAY ON BIG O. Ernest Benn, 1967; Follett, 1968.

THE PIEMAKERS. Faber and Faber, 1967; Lippincott, 1968.

A TIDE FOR THE CAPTAIN. Chatto, Boyd and Oliver, 1967.

THE BARGE CHILDREN. Brockhampton Press, 1968.

JUMBO AND THE BIG DIG. Brockhampton Press, 1968.

RUG IS A BEAR. Ernest Benn, 1968.

RUG PLAYS TRICKS. Ernest Benn, 1968.

THE SEA PIPER. Chatto, Boyd and Oliver, 1968.

THE SIGNPOSTERS. Faber and Faber, 1968.

A GAME OF CATCH. Chatto, Boyd and Oliver, 1969.

A GIFT FROM WINKLESEA. Brockhampton Press, 1969.

A HOUSE FOR JONES. Ernest Benn, 1969.

THE NIGHT-WATCHMEN. Faber and Faber, 1969; Macmillan, New York, 1970.

RUG AND A PICNIC. Ernest Benn, 1969.

RUG PLAYS BALL. Ernest Benn, 1969.

THE OUTLANDERS. Faber and Faber, 1970.

RAINBOW PAVEMENT. Ernest Benn, 1970.

THE WILKSES. B.B.C. Publications (*Jackanory series*), 1970.

THE BIRD FANCIER. Ernest Benn, 1971.

UP THE PIER. Faber and Faber, 1971.

THE WEATHER CAT. Ernest Benn, 1971.

Helen Cresswell

Short stories for children by Helen Cresswell include *Particle Goes Green* in WINTER'S TALES FOR CHILDREN 4, edited by M. R. Hodgkin (Macmillan, London, 1968) and *The Ugly Swan* in THE WORLD OF BALLET, edited by Anne Geraghty (Collins, 1970).

Meindert DeJong

Meindert DeJong was born in the village of Wierum, in Friesland, Holland, in 1906. In 1914 his family migrated to Grand Rapids, Michigan, where he was educated at local religious schools maintained by Dutch Calvinists. Later he studied at Calvin College, Michigan, and for a time at the University of Chicago. His first book, written in response to a suggestion from the children's librarian at the Grand Rapids Public Library, was The Big Goose and the Little White Duck *(1938). During the war he spent three years in China as official historian with the 14th Air Force: an experience on which* The House of Sixty Fathers *(1956) was based. He has held a variety of jobs, ranging from professor to gravedigger, bricklayer, and church janitor, and he says he finds manual labour conducive to writing.*

Mr DeJong won the 1955 Newbery Medal for The Wheel on the School. *In 1962 the International Board on Books for Young People awarded him the Hans Christian Andersen Medal, for the entire body of his work, and in 1969 he won the first National Book Award for Children's Literature with* Journey from Peppermint Street. *His books have been translated into Dutch, German, Swedish, Danish, Italian, Finnish, Japanese, Polish, Portuguese, Spanish, Czech, Slovak, Serbo-Croat, and Afrikaans.*

Meindert DeJong once defined a child as 'a small body entirely surrounded by adults'. A farm or domestic animal is similarly at the mercy of the all-powerful adults who control the scheme of things; this may be one of the many reasons for the fellow-feeling which children have with animals. The central characters of DeJong's books divide more or less equally into animals and children. He has said that, in order to recreate the world of childhood, one must go down into oneself rather than look back by way of adult memory. And this raises an obvious and not quite pointless question: how do you create the world of an animal? A writer in an American newspaper summed up the puzzle: 'When *Shadrach* [a story whose hero was a small boy] came out, we reviewers all said it was autobiographical, but now here comes *Hurry Home, Candy*, the story of a dog, and it's just as autobiographical.'

Identification, it seems to me, is both the process and the result. The author has identified with his characters, whether human or animal, and the reader in turn identifies. The imaginative leap into the animal mind is both speculative and perilous, even if—like DeJong—you restrict it to animals that you know well and for which you have deep understanding and sympathy. I am not sure that in his books it is not a two-stage process. Reading *Hurry Home, Candy*, you—whatever your chronological age—are a child feeling what it is like to be a dog. That is something we can know. What it is *really* like to be a dog is something we cannot know.

The DeJong world is solid; it is limited but large enough. Children, parents, grandparents, animals, the land: the web of relationships among these provides nearly all his settings and most of his themes. The settings divide into a Dutch landscape which he knew as a child and another which appears to be mid-Western farming country, and the external differences have their importance; but the emotional world is the same. It is a durable one. The way in which old people, old farms, old villages all recur is significant; life in these books is something that goes on, in much the same style and the same place, from one year to another; it is not a bitty, here-today-and-gone-tomorrow, contemporary urban or suburban affair. It is a life in which the Bible is known. The striking exception to the sense of permanence in DeJong's settings is *The House of Sixty Fathers* (1956), the story of a small Chinese refugee boy in the Japanese invasion, where the time dimension is suddenly cut to almost nil—a matter of whether one will eat today and escape capture tomorrow.

On the whole, DeJong's strengths and techniques are not those of the novelist, although his later books have moved a little in that direction. He does not develop individual character very far. The small boys in his books are nearly all the same small boy, although seen at different ages and in different places. His action is more often episodic than unified. He is, above all, a storyteller, especially in the early books. 'It was this way,' begins his first book, *The Big Goose and the Little White Duck*, published in 1938; 'It was like this' is the start of *The Cat That Walked a Week* (1943); 'There was this boy, Davie, and he was going to have a rabbit' are the first words of *Shadrach* (1953.) It is a speaking voice; the invitation is to gather round and listen.

DeJong does not think in terms of writing for any particular age-group, but he has written about children only up to the age of ten or eleven, and the viewpoint – if it is not that of an animal – is that of a young child. The eye-level is set simply and naturally: a gift which the author had as early as at the start of his first book, *The Big Goose*, when 'exactly at noon a big boy opened the door of the little poultry shop'. A boy, of course, appears big only to a smaller child, so we know at once what and where we are. This early book, about the goose that grumpy Grandpa was going to roast for his eighty-eighth birthday, is a pleasant piece of tale-telling, homely and repetitive, with a full supporting cast of farm animals, and with Grandpa still convincingly grumpy when at last he relents. *The Cat That Walked a Week*, about the white cat that was wickedly abducted but found its way home, is a slight, episodic story. It is a very domestic, pretty little cat, and the whole feeling of the book is catlike in a domestic, pretty way; but in spite of some superficial realism the logic is that of a modern fairy tale; and it is in answer to that logic that the people the cat has encountered on its journey all telephone in succession after it has arrived safely home, and the villains duly repent.

DeJong's writing career was diverted by the war, and it took him some years afterwards to get back on course. His first book to show exceptional promise was, to my mind, *The Tower by the Sea*, which was in fact his eighth, and was published in 1950, twelve years after *The Big Goose and the Little White Duck*. With it a deeper and darker note entered his work, for, in this story of the old woman, the blue-eyed cat and the magpie, there are forces of malice and ignorance that almost lead to a witch-burning. There is also a notable stylistic development. The sentence-construction is still simple, but the colours, sounds and associations of the words themselves are much more fully exploited, and the use of repetition is more sophisticated than before. The opening of the story is strongly pictorial:

Meindert DeJong

> In the dune village of Katverloren there once was a cradle on the tower. On the cradle was a cat. The white enamelled cat on the cradle stood with uplifted paw, pointing the direction of the wind. The white cat on the tower had a big blue jewel for its eye. It was as blue as a sea full of sunshine.
>
> It is all gone now . . .

And the sound effects can be equally striking: for instance, in the description of the magpie.

> Always it was full of wild plans and wicked mischief. Always it went about chattering to itself. Always busy. Too busy. Always talking about nothing. Pesky and busy and wicked and noisy.

For all its bright detail, this is a *tale*: from long ago; distanced. It is based, I believe, on a North Sea legend. It has the air of being half-remembered, half-reconstructed; confidently told but without giving or needing any guarantee of accuracy. How close it is to the legend's received form I do not know and have not inquired, because it does not matter.

Shadrach (1953) is the story of Davie and the little black rabbit, 'fairest of ten thousand to my soul'. I do not know of any comparable exploration of a child's longing, except perhaps in Philippa Pearce's *A Dog So Small.* It takes half the length of the book before the long-awaited Shadrach arrives; then he is lost, and is found in the room where Grandpa keeps the gear from his old, nostalgically-recalled days as fisherman and canal-boatman. Davie is still delicate after illness; and behind the story of his yearning for the rabbit is the concern of parents and grandparents for his own health. But obsession and disappointment and anxiety are not all; the book also expresses joy; and the expression of joy is a notable DeJong quality.

DeJong's Newbery award-winning book, *The Wheel on the School* (1954), is his best known up to the present, though perhaps not his best. Structurally it is more interesting than the others. It begins as quietly as any book could start, with the reading of a child's essay in school. The six children in the one-and-only class consider Lina's observation that no storks come to their North

Sea village; decide that the roofs are too sharp and that they need, as in other villages, a wagon wheel for the storks to nest on; and set out separately to find one. The story follows first one child, then another, gradually gathering speed and building up to a series of climaxes in the perils of sea and storm. As it progresses, more and more members of the community are brought in until the whole village is involved in retrieving and erecting the cartwheel that will bring storks to Shora. The scale of the action, in which lives are risked at least three times, is not too great in symbolic terms, because storks are bearers of good fortune and guardians of family life. But in literal terms, one wonders whether a sensible Dutch community would not have been more cautious.

The House of Sixty Fathers is the Odyssey of a small Chinese boy, swept away down river from his parents in a sampan during the Japanese invasion of China. This is a story of continual action; harrowing, more unified, more of a novel than most of DeJong's work; and it is a story that, without a didactic word, impresses on the reader the pity and terror of war. But these terms, which in one way can be used to commend it, in another way must be used to qualify one's praise. It is a value-laden story whose very humanity seems to have slightly weighed down the creative imagination, and it does not reach the heights one might have hoped for.

Of the animal books, the most notable probably is *Along Came a Dog* (1958), about the friendship of a stray dog and a little red hen. This story, in which no child character sets foot, catches the drama of the barnyard and gives life even to the unpromising inhabitants of the chicken-run. No other writer can ever have made such a likeable individual out of a hen. But the DeJong books which appeal most strongly to me are not, for all their merits, either the animal stories or the heavyweights of the middle period like *The House of Sixty Fathers* and *The Wheel on the School*. His talent, I believe, has been at its best in two stories about children and parents published during the 1960s: *The Singing Hill* (1962) and *Far Out the Long Canal* (1964). In these books the family relationships are precisely and sensitively noted, and the moments of swift childlike delight in being alive are most vividly conveyed.

The Singing Hill is a book with an American setting: in deep country, among miles of cornland. Small in the middle of this vastness is the youngest child of a family, isolated when the older two move away into the busy new world of school, when father is away all week and mother endlessly occupied. Only young Ray himself has nothing important to do. He finds that outside the family there are others who suffer from the lack of a rôle: the old man he calls Grandpa, who is old and feeble, and the horse that has finished its useful life and that Ray eventually manages to bring down to the stable adjoining his house. But what lights up the book is an occasional sense of sheer joy; for, after all, this is the natural order of things and the land is fruitful.

> The little hills rejoice on every side.
> The pastures are clothed with flocks;
> The valleys are covered over with corn;
> They shout for joy, they also sing.

'Say it again,' urges Ray, when his mother quotes these words of the Psalmist. But he can't wait. He runs out to play in the lane.

The setting of *Far Out the Long Canal* is again Holland. Moonta's obsession is learning to skate; and when he does learn, his skates take him, contrary to orders, miles along the melting ice of the canal, where fortunately he can help to bring Father and Grandfather safely home. There is a brilliant sense of cold, crisp, sparkling festival when the whole village is out on the ice. Comparisons with *Hans Brinker* are unavoidable, and to my mind they are all in DeJong's favour.

Journey from Peppermint Street (1968) is the strangest of all the books. Siebren's trip through the Friesland villages and across the marsh by night to the monastery-farmhouse of his tiny aunt and huge deaf-and-dumb uncle has in it something of the traditional Quest. And there is much else; it is a story full of echoes, hints, implications. But there is also something uncomfortable, a slightly cloying sweetness about the relationships of Siebren with grown-ups. This is a characteristic found from time to time in other books, too. Mothers are always there and caring, fathers are 'sure as the dike and strong as the church', grandparents are wise if occasionally a shade crotchety. Children are suffused from time to time with love for their elders. There's a good home for every stray.

A Sense of Story

When the first National Book Award for children's literature was made to Meindert DeJong for *Journey from Peppermint Street* in the spring of 1969, there was criticism of the choice as conventional and unimaginative. I have some sympathy with the critics. One would always like an important new award to go to a new writer with new things to say. DeJong's abilities are well known and have been widely recognized. But a valid criticism of an award is not necessarily a valid criticism of the recipient. DeJong is a limited and rather old-fashioned writer whose main springs of inspiration clearly come from a childhood which itself was a good many years ago. He is an adequate technician, as you would expect of a man who has published a score of books, but not a brilliant stylist. His books are bread, not cake; but they are none the worse for that. There is no reason to suppose that he is finished; he has still been breaking new ground in recent work; but it does not now seem too soon to look at his achievement as a whole. He seems to me to have two remarkable talents which justify his career and the honours he has received. One is that of achieving an extraordinary empathy with children and animals; the other is that of expressing joy. And the latter is one of the rarest gifts of all. Come and go what may, there is always room for joy.

Here is an extract from Meindert DeJong's Newbery Award acceptance speech in 1955:

To get back to [the essence of childhood] you can only go down. You can only go in—deep in. Down through all the deep, mystic, intuitive layers of the subconscious back into your own childhood. And if you go deep enough, get basic enough, become again the child you were, it seems reasonable that by way of the subconscious you have come into what must be the universal child. Then, and then only, do you write for the child.

To me the downward, inward way of the subconscious is the only way, because it is eternally true that you can't go back—you can't ever go back anywhere—and least of all into childhood. You may try to go back by way of memory, but that memory is an adult memory, an adult conception of childhood for adults—and not for children . . . When you write for children from adult memory, you satisfy only the other adults who have also forgotten their inner childhood, and have substituted for it an adult conception of what the child needs and wants in books.

And in his National Book Award acceptance speech in 1969 Mr DeJong said:

The separate world of the child is a brief world because it is a world of wonder . . . But where does wonder go? In a few brief years it is stultified into adulthood. And its duration is shortened all the more because adults are eternally—maybe necessarily—busy making the child adult and like unto themselves . . .

In terms of adult experience, the child's world and the world of children's literature are limited worlds. But it is in that very limitation that the writer for children finds his joy and his challenge and his untrammelled creativity. Braque said it right for painting; I say it after him for children's literature: 'Limitation of means determines style, engenders form and new form, and gives impulse to creativity.'

These absolutes must be kept in mind when reaching as an adult author into the important separateness of the child's world. I am not, and must not be, aware of my audience when I write my books. I must be wholly subjective, conscious only of the particular limiting cage of form of the children's book into which I must shape and compress my creation. After some twenty books, I still have no idea of the age, school grade, and state of literacy of the child for whom I write. I write not only out of myself but also for myself, necessarily shaping the work only to my particular cage of artistic form.

Meindert DeJong

Bibliography

THE BIG GOOSE AND THE LITTLE WHITE DUCK. Harper and Row, 1938; Lutterworth Press, 1964.

DIRK'S DOG BELLO. Harper and Row, 1939; Lutterworth Press, 1960.

BELLS OF THE HARBOR. Harper and Row, 1941.

WHEELS OVER THE BRIDGE. Harper and Row, 1941.

THE CAT THAT WALKED A WEEK. Harper and Row, 1943; Lutterworth Press, 1965.

THE LITTLE STRAY DOG. Harper and Row, 1943.

BILLY AND THE UNHAPPY BULL. Harper and Row, 1946; Lutterworth Press, 1966.

GOOD LUCK DUCK. Harper and Row, 1950.

THE TOWER BY THE SEA. Harper and Row, 1950; Lutterworth Press, 1964.

SMOKE ABOVE THE LANE. Harper and Row, 1951.

HURRY HOME, CANDY. Harper and Row, 1953; Lutterworth Press, 1962.

SHADRACH. Harper and Row, 1953; Lutterworth Press, 1957.

THE WHEEL ON THE SCHOOL. Harper and Row, 1954; Lutterworth Press, 1956.

THE LITTLE COW AND THE TURTLE. Harper and Row, 1955; Lutterworth Press, 1961.

THE HOUSE OF SIXTY FATHERS. Harper and Row, 1956; Lutterworth Press, 1958.

ALONG CAME A DOG. Harper and Row, 1958; Lutterworth Press, 1959.

THE MIGHTY ONES: GREAT MEN AND WOMEN OF EARLY BIBLE DAYS. Harper and Row, 1959; Lutterworth Press, 1960.

THE LAST LITTLE CAT. Harper and Row, 1961; Lutterworth Press, 1962.

NOBODY PLAYS WITH A CABBAGE. Harper and Row, 1962; Lutterworth Press, 1963.

THE SINGING HILL. Harper and Row, 1962; Lutterworth Press, 1963.

FAR OUT THE LONG CANAL. Harper and Row, 1964; Lutterworth Press, 1965.

PUPPY SUMMER. Harper and Row, 1966; Lutterworth Press, 1966.

JOURNEY FROM PEPPERMINT STREET. Harper and Row, 1968; Lutterworth Press, 1969.

A HORSE CAME RUNNING. Macmillan, New York, 1970; Lutterworth Press, 1970.

THE EASTER CAT. Macmillan, New York, 1971; Lutterworth Press, 1971.

Eleanor Estes

Eleanor Estes was born in 1906 at West Haven, Connecticut. On finishing high school she went to work in the children's department of the New Haven Free Public Library. In 1931 she was awarded the Caroline M. Hewins scholarship for outstanding work as a children's librarian, and went to New York to study at the Pratt Institute library school. She married Rice Estes, then a student at the school, in 1932. Until 1940 she worked in the children's rooms of the New York Public Library. Her books for children include three about the Moffat family: The Moffats, The Middle Moffat, *and* Rufus M; *two about the Pyes:* Ginger Pye *and* Pinky Pye; *and* The Witch Family, *all of which have been published in England as well as the United States. She has also written adult novels.* Ginger Pye *won the Newbery Medal in 1952.*

Writing for children does not always, or even usually, require the author to take a child's-eye view. The mark of the tenth-rate story for children is often a creaking attempt to get down to child level, like an uncle on hands and knees playing games on the carpet. It is ineffectual and undignified. Children, on the whole, prefer adults to behave as adults, and to talk to them as adults talk. Yet the story of family life, which can be weighed by the child against his own experience in a way that the fairy tale or adventure story cannot, does require of its author a lively sense of what it is like to be a child in a family.

Although most of us see children from outside on most days of the week, I believe it is true that to *feel* as a child we must usually rely on the still-existent child within ourselves. It was not by accident that Louisa Alcott, and even E. Nesbit, who had several children of her own, went back to memories of their own childhood. Among living writers, Meindert DeJong and Noel Streatfeild have drawn on similar resources. And Eleanor Estes, in her books on the Moffats and the Pyes, went back to the place and period, and many of the details, of her own youth in a small Connecticut town. The quality of the three Moffat books which makes them exceptional is, I think, an unusual purity of the childish vision. This is not to say that the books themselves are childish. The author has the gift of selective recall, combined with adult experience of work with children, and with the mature qualities of perception and perspective. She has also a limpid, apparently effortless style which suggests a natural writer.

A natural writer; not, I think, a born novelist. Mrs Estes's books for children have been artistically successful in inverse proportion to the extent to which they employed, or needed to employ, the novelist's technique.

The three Moffat books are not novels. Yet although they seem artless they are perfectly formed. Each book consists of a chain of episodes, linked unobtrusively by a theme which requires little development and imparts little tension; and this is exactly the construction which allows the author to make the best use of her talents. In *Ginger Pye* and *The Alley*, however, there are plots of mystery and detection which call for a dramatic build-up, a logical progression towards climax, which the author is infuriatingly unable or unwilling to provide.

Ginger Pye (1951) is the story of the kidnapping and recovery of Ginger, the 'pure-bred, part fox-terrier and part collie' pup whom Jerry and Rachel Pye have saved up to buy. And as a story it hangs fire for chapter after chapter. Even the climax is more of an anticlimax, since Jerry's and Rachel's attempts at detection are hardly relevant and Ginger escapes by his own efforts, aided by the quickness of Uncle Bennie, aged three. Similarly in *The Alley* (1964) the investigation of a double crime, committed by burglars and by supposed policemen, proceeds so slowly that the reader experiences impatience rather than suspense. As stories of detection by youngsters, these do not begin to compare with the work of such writers as Erich Kästner and Paul Berna.

But *Ginger Pye* at least is not to be judged as a failed mystery story. It is a much-liked and likeable book whose merits have little to do with its plot. (The trouble probably is that the plot is not of a *kind* which can be successfully faded into the background; it demands to be developed.) The real interest of the story lies in the characters of the Pye family and in the irrelevant or barely-relevant episodes which are forever pushing the story-line aside.

Mrs Estes has said that Rachel and Jerry, who are nine and ten at the start of the story, are based on 'all the children I've ever known', which seems to suggest that they are composite characters rather than individuals. This may be true of Jerry, a sturdy small boy who is quite credible but has no marked personality of his own. But it cannot be true of Rachel, who has an interesting, quirky mind and an endearing habit of slipping away into by-ways of reminiscence. And there are oddly memorable incidents: no reader of *Ginger Pye* will surely ever forget how Mr Pye met Mrs Pye by knocking her down when he was trying to run up the down escalator, or how Rachel and Jerry polished the pews in church with three-year-old Uncle Bennie's help:

> Rachel had quite a long duster, and she tied it around Uncle Bennie's pants. 'Whee-ee,' she said, sending him sliding down the long pew . . .
>
> And, 'Whee-ee,' said Jerry, picking him up, putting him on the next pew and sending him sliding back.
>
> This was great fun for everybody and particularly for Uncle Bennie, who thought it almost as good as tobogganing. He did not mind at all being turned into a duster.

The characters of the mild ornithologist Mr Pye and of poor worried Mama are rounded out in a sequel, *Pinky Pye* (1958), which brings two new members to the Pye family: a small clever kitten and a small fierce owl. And there are further engaging glimpses of Uncle Bennie, cherishing his pet the dead locust, or conversing with God and obligingly replying to himself on behalf of the Almighty. Uncle Bennie and Pinky Pye herself, the kitten who can type – for did she not produce before witnesses the word *woogie* on the typewriter? – make the book worth while, although the meditations of Pinky with which we are presented do not strike me as kittenlike.

Among Mrs Estes's books of the 1960s, *The Witch Family*, in which two small girls become more and more involved in an imaginary world which they themselves have created, is an interesting conception but it doesn't come off; one feels that even in fictional terms nothing is really happening. *The Alley*—in the intervals between the author's attempts to make something of its burglar-catching plot—is more successful, perhaps because it is closer to the kind of thing she can do best. The Alley is a small Brooklyn backwater occupied by academic families; and in it Mrs Estes creates a whole community of children, every one distinct. The characters include a charmingly loquacious ten-year-old heroine, Connie, and the formidable, law-giving Katy who keeps the whole place in order. There is a splendidly funny chapter—quite irrelevant to the story—in which Connie sets up the Alley Conservatory of Music and offers piano lessons to the other children. Her first pupil is Winifred.

> 'Now,' said Connie, plunging right into lesson one, not to lose any time. 'You see those gold letters in the middle of the piano. They say, "Ludlow". Now, middle C is just a little bit to the left of the centre of those gold letters. That is the way to find C, the most important note of the piano. If you have that, you have everything. Now, I will play the scale of C major.'
>
> Connie played the scale of C major. She decided that she might be a piano teacher when she grew up, because she enjoyed teaching so much.

The next pupil is Nicky, who is only three but comes in for some praise:

> 'You have a very good ear,' said Connie.
> 'Yes,' he said. 'I can wiggle it.'

In spite of its unsatisfactory story-line, I am sorry that *The Alley* has not so far been published in England. There are several episodes which prove that the author has by no means lost her touch. Yet it is still the three Moffat books which show Mrs Estes at her best. She has never surpassed them; they are the heart of her achievement.

The Moffats, The Middle Moffat and *Rufus M* were published in the United States in the early 1940s but did not reach England until nearly twenty years later. They tell of incidents in the life of a hard-up family in the New England town of 'Cranbury'—

very close to New Haven – just before and during the First World War. When written they were already period pieces, with their references to horse-drawn wagons and early, spluttering automobiles, old-fashioned clothes and furnishings and habits. But their appeal is not a period appeal: it is the enduring essence of childhood.

At the start, Sylvie Moffat is fifteen, Joey twelve, Jane nine and Rufus five and a half. Mama, a widow, is a dressmaker. Some three years appear to pass during the three books. The point of view is almost always that of the younger members of the family; neither Mama nor Sylvie is ever the central character of an episode, and Joey stars very rarely. The threat of sale hanging over the family home is the thread that holds the episodes of the first book together; the second book, *The Middle Moffat*, is loosely threaded by Jane's efforts to see the Oldest Inhabitant safely through to his hundredth birthday; the third, with Rufus as hero, has the First World War as its background.

The style is simple, never arch or facetious. But the author is not afraid to make her hero or heroine the victim of gentle humour, so that, at the same time as identifying, the child can also stand outside and patronize. The humour has even a slight dryness. When we learn that 'My Country, 'Tis of Thee' was all Rufus could play on the organ, we are also told, casually, that he could play it like lightning. And 'Fine! Fine! Just what I've always wanted,' says the Oldest Inhabitant, on being told his fortune, which is, 'The world is your oyster. You will be a fireman.' Again and again there is the contrast between children's wild ambitions and what they can actually do; and the details they worry about in their grandiose schemes are – convincingly – mere gnats to be strained at when the camel is already swallowed. Thus Rufus, convinced that with a little practice he can become an expert ventriloquist, plans to project Harold Callahan's voice into Harold Callahan's inkwell at school and shout 'Let me out!'; but he feels he will have to be sure the sliding lid on Harold's inkwell is open, 'because he was not certain a ventriloquist could throw his voice into an inkwell if the top was closed'.

The small, precise touch, evoking at once the response that 'yes, it was like that', is a recurrent feature of all three books, beginning with the first sentence of *The Moffats*, which shows Jane marvelling at the way Mama can peel apples so rapidly into long ringlets. The title of *Rufus M* derives from Rufus's attempt to fill out a library card; the M was as far as he could get in the available space, and every child and parent knows just how that happened. Joey Moffat, we are told, 'always had a good pencil with a fine sharp point in his pocket. He could whistle and he could whittle.' Yes, of course, he would. He was that kind of boy. 'But he was not good at dancing school and he did not like it.' No, of course, he wouldn't.

A fact seldom emphasized but often indicated is that the Moffats are poor. For Mama—and, increasingly, big sister Sylvie—family life means work and worry as well as love. This is a feature in common with *Little Women* and with E. Nesbit's Bastable stories and *The Railway Children*. The efforts to save or earn a few pennies, the horror when a five-dollar bill seems lost, are serious matters; the solidarity of the family counts for a great deal when the wolf is not all that far from the door. Against a background of material poverty, the wealth of family affection can be seen at its true value.

Two episodes, both in *Rufus M*—the last of the three books—stand a little apart from the rest. One is Rufus's end-of-season visit to the mist-wreathed pleasure-ground, which has an air of wistful strangeness. The other is the final chapter, in which the Moffats' plans and dreams float up the chimney on scraps of charred paper. This last is one of the very few occasions on which I think an ending is acceptable for children which one might not offer to adults. To a grown-up person this scene seems slightly contrived and sentimental. But grown-ups are sophisticated in the matter of story design; also, we are afraid of our feelings. In this case, the occasion is the farewell to a family whom the reader has come to know well in the course of the three books, and to love greatly. The note is a proper one on which to end; it rings true. If it is embarrassing to grown-ups, that may be a reflection on grown-ups rather than on children or on the author.

The Moffat books are, I believe, outstanding among family stories. On them, with a little support from the Pyes and *The Alley*, Mrs Estes's reputation rests. It is quite a small base. But in the last analysis a writer's distinction does not depend on the number of his books, or even on the number of his good books. It depends on the quality of his best. Three like those about the Moffats are sufficient.

The following extracts are reproduced with permission from a talk given by Mrs Estes in New York to a meeting of the International Reading Association:

Like bees who by instinct go from flower to flower gathering honey, writers, merely by being alive, are constantly gathering ideas and impressions—their honey—which eventually will lodge somewhere in some book. To bees, some honey is sweeter than other, and some quite bitter. Yet, bitter or sweet, it is all gathered, and so it is with the born writer that all ideas and impressions are his potential nectar and must be gathered and stored by him, either to be used in a book, rejected, or held in reserve.

There are probably as many ways of writing a book as there are writers, and each individual has his own means, stemming from his own personality, of conveying ideas and impressions, so no two people could write the same book. Today I speak only for myself when I speak of how a book gets written. Sometimes I feel I am a blindfolded person and groping my way toward a book. Then I pick up the scent of the book and happily I am on my way, the trail of the book having become clear, direct, and straight. I am the sort of writer who would like to have plenty of time in which to do nothing. Time just to sit, or to stand at the window, or watch the ocean, or people, or to wander up the street or about the house, to pace. For often it is in these do-nothing times that the best honey is gathered. 'How many hours a day does the writer spend upon his book?' is a question often asked. 'Twenty-four,' the answer could be, for does not the writer call upon his dreams? And unlike the bee, who has to go and get his honey, the writer need never stir from one spot; his honey comes to him . . .

To the writer, his memory and his impressions are insistent. He finds he must get them down on paper, enhance them in the light of his own imagination, use them as a springboard. This happens often years and years after the impression has been made . . .

In writing, inventiveness and imagination become partners of remembered impressions, and all skip along together. 'Now you, now me,' they seem to say, none of them alone being sufficient for creating a book. In revising a book, which I do many times, sometimes a thought or an incident is taken out and put back into storage. If it is worth writing about, it will emerge again some other time while writing some other book and insist upon being included. With each writing of his book, the writer is like a singer striving, pushing, reaching higher for a still higher, and more eloquent, note. Now the intellectual concept, the conscious thinking about what has been emerging, outweighs the first outpouring. The writer must survey his work critically, coolly, and as though he were a stranger to it. He must be willing to prune, expertly and hardheartedly. At the end of each revision, a manuscript may look like a battered old hive, worked over, torn apart, pinned together, added to, deleted from, words changed and words changed back. Yet the book must retain its initial freshness and spontaneity.

It is only after the fourth revision that I feel I know my book. It takes a while to get used to the new book. The writer is a little shaken and uncertain for a time. Is the book, most of all, a good one? Was the best, most flavoursome honey put into it? How much a writer needs to be told now, 'How beautiful!' when, finally, his book is off to the press; how lost he feels without it, having grown now to love it.

Eleanor Estes

Bibliography

THE MOFFATS. Harcourt Brace, 1941; The Bodley Head, 1959.

THE MIDDLE MOFFAT. Harcourt Brace, 1942; The Bodley Head, 1960.

THE SUN AND THE WIND AND MR TODD. Harcourt Brace, 1943.

RUFUS M. Harcourt Brace, 1943; The Bodley Head, 1960.

THE HUNDRED DRESSES. Harcourt Brace, 1944.

THE SLEEPING GIANT, AND OTHER STORIES. Harcourt Brace, 1948.

GINGER PYE. Harcourt Brace, 1951; The Bodley Head, 1961.

A LITTLE OVEN. Harcourt Brace, 1955.

PINKY PYE. Harcourt Brace, 1958; Longman, 1959.

THE WITCH FAMILY. Harcourt Brace, 1960; Longman, 1962.

THE ALLEY. Harcourt Brace, 1964.

MIRANDA THE GREAT. Harcourt Brace, 1967.

THE LOLIPOP PRINCESS: A PLAY FOR PAPER DOLLS IN ONE ACT. Harcourt Brace, 1967.

Paula Fox

Paula Fox was born in New York City. Her mother was Spanish, her father a writer, Paul Harvey Fox. She has two sons and lives in Brooklyn with her husband, who is a professor. She has written short stories, television plays and adult novels in addition to her books for children, which include How Many Miles to Babylon? *(1967),* The Stone-Faced Boy *(1968) and* Portrait of Ivan *(1969).*

Paula Fox, like Meindert DeJong and Eleanor Estes, has usually made children from about seven to ten years old her main characters. But whereas one would say fairly confidently that DeJong and Mrs Estes have written *for* this age-group as well as about it, Paula Fox leaves everything in doubt. She has written both adult and children's novels, and she does not claim to understand what constitutes the difference between them. Like many other writers, she raises the question 'For whom?', and as with many other writers I can find no answer except 'For whom it may concern'.

Miss Fox's worlds are either sharp and precise or deliberately drifting and shadowy, and for English children whose ideas of American daily life are formed largely by television they may be difficult worlds in which to become acclimatized. The books have an air of newness: not merely the kind of contemporaneity which almost anyone can achieve but the newness that comes from looking at things with new eyes, feeling them in a new way.

Miss Fox is of a younger generation than DeJong and Mrs Estes. And whereas to them childhood is a mainly happy time that fits naturally into the family-life pattern of youth, middle age and old age, a recurrent theme of Paula Fox is that of non-communication and lack of understanding between young and old. It is not the generation gap, exactly, but Miss Fox lives in the world we know at our nerve-ends, in which the old comfortable certainties can no longer be relied on.

The audience, and the writer's position in relation to it, seem indeed as fluid as everything else about Paula Fox's work. One has no sense that the writer, an adult, is *here*, in charge, handing it out, while the audience of children is *there*, duly taking it. If there is a message in the air it is probably for someone quite different. Miss Fox's first two books for children, *Maurice's Room* and *A Likely Place*, are not telling children anything except a story, but seem rather obviously to be saying something to parents: don't fuss the child, let him grow in his own way. The two books are humorous, even witty, but in a way that one would expect to appeal to children rather older than their heroes who are eight and nine respectively – or to adults. And her best book, *How Many Miles to Babylon?*, whose hero is barely ten, is one of only two books specifically recommended for teenagers in an article by Nat Hentoff in *The Atlantic* for December 1967. The conventional wisdom is that children and teenagers don't want to read about those younger than themselves, and this generally appears to be true. But it could be that discussion on the question betrays a more fixed attitude than Paula Fox would adopt. Who says who is to read what; who says that grown-ups have all the wisdom anyway?

Maurice's Room (1966) is, in fact, a blessedly funny book; and as for readership, one can only try it on and see if the glove fits. Maurice at eight is dedicated to his collection of junk, which spills over everything. His parents feel he needs more constructive interests, and often discuss him with their friends.

> Some visitors said that collections like Maurice's showed that a child would become a great scientist. Many great scientists had collected junk when they were eight years old. Other visitors said Maurice would outgrow his collection and become interested in other things, such as money or armies. Some suggested to the Henrys that they ought to buy Maurice a dog, or send him to music school so that his time might be spent more usefully.

And his parents, with the best intentions, get everything wrong. The dog they borrow to be a companion to Maurice is in fact a dreadful nuisance to him, yet Mother is soon convinced that 'Maurice and Patsy are inseparable'. An attempt to get Maurice to learn an instrument is disastrous. The beautiful sailboat that Mr Henry buys Maurice for his birthday is forgotten while Maurice and friend grope for some old bedsprings lying on the bottom of the pond. 'If I had known you wanted bedsprings instead of a beautiful three-foot sailing ketch, I would have gotten you bedsprings,' says poor Mr Henry in despair. Finally, Maurice's parents decide to move to the country, where they hope that everything will be different. And this time at least all is well, for although Maurice isn't terribly interested in the country as such, there is an old barn that already holds the nucleus of a promising new junk collection. It's an hilarious, subversive book, full of casual joys, as when Maurice's mother lets his uncle in at the front door:

> 'Well, Lily, how are you?'
> 'Fine, and you?'
> 'Fine, and your husband?'
> 'Fine, and Patsy?'
> 'Fine."
> 'Fine,' said Maurice to the hamster.
> 'And how is Maurice?' asked the uncle.
> 'Fine,' said his mother.
> 'He'll be delighted to see Patsy.'
> 'He surely will be delighted.'

But Maurice isn't.

Lewis, in *A Likely Place* (1967), is fussed by the grown-ups too, but is fortunately left by his parents in the charge of eccentric Miss Fitchlow, who goes in for yogurt and yoga, calls Lewis 'pal', and lets him off the lead. Which is just what he needed. It is a short, dry, subtle book; and if there is a lesson in it, then I suspect that, as in *Maurice's Room*, it is really a lesson for parents.

Paula Fox's reputation at the time of writing, however, rests largely on her third book, *How Many Miles to Babylon?* (1967). This is a longer novel of much greater depth and complexity. Its hero, James, is a small black boy living in Brooklyn, whose father has disappeared and whose mother has gone into hospital, leaving him in the care of three elderly aunts. One day he walks out of school and goes to play by himself in an empty house. In his mind is a story that his mother has really gone to her own country across the seas and that he is secretly a prince. Three small boys, not much older than James but tougher, capture him and make him help them work their dog-stealing racket. James travels frightening miles with them on the back of a bicycle, goes to a deserted funhouse on Coney Island, sees the Atlantic. At night he frees the stolen dogs, runs away, gets home to the old aunts, and finds his mother there. She is back from hospital; she is no princess and he no prince. 'Hello, Jimmy,' she says.

On the surface it is a straightforward story, with its strong plot about the fearful boy and the tough gang and the dogs and the juvenile racketeering. But there are strange undertones: the symbolic voyage, the 'other' story of James which is only hinted at. The action, although shadows are cast before and behind it in time, takes place within a day and a night. 'Can I get there by candlelight? Yes, and back again.' Both action and setting are almost dreamlike; the landscape an intimately-known landscape yet glimpsed as if in shifting mists. Everything is experienced through James; and James himself is wandering in a mist of illusion, though eventually compelled by what happens to grasp at rough reality. It is felt in every page, but never said in crude terms, that James is a member of a submerged race and class, and isolated even within that. He is not a sharply-drawn character, nor meant to be, for the reader will suffer with him rather than observe him from the outside; but the minor characters – the three old aunts, the three young racketeers – are clear in outline, defined by the words they speak.

In one sense the outcome of *How Many Miles to Babylon?* is plain. James has proved himself, has faced the actual world, found and accepted his actual mother. He has come through. But to say that is not enough. Illusion and reality, the symbolic and the actual, are not to be so neatly separated. There is much in the book that the mind cannot simply deal with and eject; much that stays around. The inner mystery is something to be carried about and wondered at from time to time rather than resolved.

The same might be said of *The Stone-Faced Boy* (1968), whose hero Gus – the middle child of five, about ten years old, timid, vulnerable, shut-off – goes out into the snow at night to free a stray dog from a trap. Gus, too, proves himself; finds the key that will help him to overcome his problems. But again this is not all. *The Stone-Faced Boy* is a winter's tale, with the quiet, real-yet-unreal feeling of a white landscape. There is a shiver in it, too; a ghostliness. The trap in which the dog is caught belongs to an old man, who takes Gus home to his cottage, full of the debris of the past, for a cup of tea with his equally old wife. And at one point the old man tells the old lady to show Gus how spry she is:

> She made a strange little jump and then, holding her skirt out with her two hands, she did a little dance in front of the stove, smiling, wobbling slightly, kicking one foot out, then the other. Then she fell back softly into the rocker, like a feather coming to rest.

On the previous page we have heard that the old lady 'had a light, free laugh, and to Gus's surprise the sound reminded him of Serena'. Serena is his younger sister, aged about eight: nice, dreamy, imaginative. Gus feels it is impossible for Serena to get so old. (But of course she will.)

Of Miss Fox's remaining books for children, it seems to me that three are of rather limited interest. *Dear Prosper* (1968) is the first person story of a dog's life; it represents a literary genre of respectable antiquity, but in itself is quite ordinary. *The King's Falcon* (1969) is a slight, apparently allegorical fairytale about a king who seeks to be free of his kingdom. *Hungry Fred*, published in the same year, is a way-out picture-book about a boy who eats his way through the contents of the house, the house itself, and the back-yard, and is still hungry. Then he makes friends with a wild rabbit as big as himself. 'The rabbit leaned against Fred. Fred smiled. He felt full.' Adult readers aware of Miss Fox's preoccupations may guess what she is getting at; to children the book can only be baffling. And although one accepts that a picture-book, like a poem or story, does not have to be understood in literal terms in order to make its impact, there needs to be an imaginative power and unity which I do not find in *Hungry Fred* and which the artist, understandably, could not supply.

Portrait of Ivan (1969) is more substantial and to my mind more successful than any of these, although it does not have the mysterious depths of *How Many Miles to Babylon?* or *The Stone-Faced Boy*. It is a brief novel about a boy of eleven who leads a dull, lonely life, walled in by well-to-do, conventional, adult-dominated surroundings.

The walls around him begin to crack when he meets the painter Matt and the elderly reader-aloud Miss Manderby, and start collapsing rapidly as he potters about in a boat with a barefoot girl called Geneva. There is a key sentence to the understanding of one aspect of Paula Fox when Ivan realizes that in his life in the city

> he was nearly always being taken to or from some place by an adult, in nearly every moment of his day he was holding onto a rope held at the other end by a grown-up person – a teacher or a bus driver, a housekeeper or a relative. But since he had met Matt, space had been growing all around him. It was frightening to let go of that rope, but it made him feel light and quick instead of heavy and slow.

Paula Fox is obviously much concerned with relationships between children and adults. She is conscious that in a complicated and changing society it is hard for the generations to live together satisfactorily. In her books the 'good' grown-ups are the flexible ones who appreciate the variousness of things and people, who do not think in terms of feeding a child into the production line and in due course drawing off an adult from the other end.

She is a very individual writer; and in view of this and an uncertainty about whom her books are trying to speak to, I would expect her to be a minority taste. I would not be nearly as confident of a child's liking Paula Fox as of his liking Meindert DeJong or Eleanor Estes. But the minority has its rights and is worth extending. Some of Miss Fox's books – most notably *How Many Miles to Babylon?* and *The Stone-Faced Boy* – are of striking quality and offer a kind of literary experience which is not too common in children's books. If they are read they will not be quickly forgotten.

Paula Fox writes:

My career sounds like flap copy of the 1930s. The strangest, but not the worst, job I ever had was punctuating Italian madrigals of the fifteenth century. I assume my employer thought my guess was as good as his. I worked in Europe for a year, for Victor Gollancz, then as a string reporter for a news agency. I've taught school for seven years, sold two television plays, written two novels for grown-ups. I started writing late by most standards, I guess. Now I can't seem to stop.

I never think I'm writing for children, when I work. A story does not start *for* anyone, nor an idea, nor a feeling of an idea; but starts more for oneself . . . I think any story is a metaphor. It is not life. There is no way out but to pick a glove that conforms most to the hand. But the glove is never the hand, only a shape. And a child's hand is not an adult's. So, of course, I do write for children, *or* for adults. But the connection between them, the differences even, don't seem to me to be really relevant, only talking-points. What applies to good writing is, I think, absolute, whether for children or grown-ups, or the blind or the deaf or the thin or the fat . . . I am just starting another children's book and another novel—and I hope I shall remember which is which.

Paula Fox

Bibliography

Books for children:

MAURICE'S ROOM. Macmillan, New York, 1966.

A LIKELY PLACE. Macmillan, New York, 1967; Macmillan, London, 1968.

HOW MANY MILES TO BABYLON? David White, 1967; Macmillan, London, 1968.

DEAR PROSPER. David White, 1968.

THE STONE-FACED BOY. Bradbury Press, 1968; Macmillan, London, 1969.

HUNGRY FRED. Bradbury Press, 1969.

THE KING'S FALCON. Bradbury Press, 1969.

PORTRAIT OF IVAN. Bradbury Press, 1969; Macmillan, London, 1970.

BLOWFISH LIVE IN THE SEA. Bradbury Press, 1970.

Leon Garfield

Leon Garfield was born in Brighton in 1921. He was for a time an art student before joining the Army and serving for five years of the Second World War in England, Belgium, and Germany. He worked for some years after the war as a hospital biochemist, but is now a full-time writer. His books include Jack Holborn *(1964);* Devil-in-the-Fog *(1966), which was the first winner of the* Guardian *award for children's fiction;* Smith *(1967), a runner-up for the Carnegie Medal and Arts Council award winner;* Black Jack *(1968), again a Carnegie Medal runner-up; and* The Drummer Boy *(1970). He lives in Highgate, London, with his wife and daughter.*

Of all the talents that emerged in the field of British writing for children in the 1960s, that of Leon Garfield seems to me to be the richest and strangest. I am tempted to go on and say that his stories are the tallest, the deepest, the wildest, the most spine-chilling, the most humorous, the most energetic, the most extravagant, the most searching, the most everything. Superlatives sit as naturally on them as a silk hat on T. S. Eliot's Bradford millionaire. They are vastly larger, livelier and more vivid than life. They are intensely individual: it would be impossible to mistake a page of Garfield for a page written by anybody else. They are full of outward and visible action, but they are not just chains of events, for everything that happens on the surface has its powerful motivation beneath. And they create their own probabilities. Wildly unlikely it may be that the waif Smith should be rewarded with ten thousand guineas by the not-conspicuously-generous heirs to a fortune, but like many farther-fetched events this is entirely acceptable because nothing less would have matched the size of the story.

Although Garfield is endlessly versatile within his range, the range itself is narrow. His novels so far are all set in the eighteenth century, mostly in London and southern England.

His themes are few and recurrent: mysteries of origin and identity; the deceptive appearances of good and evil; contrasts of true and false feeling; the precarious survival of compassion and charity in a tempestuous world. His characters, though never cardboard, are seldom of great psychological complexity as we understand the phrase these days, and often themselves appear to represent underlying forces or passions or even humours.

The choice of the eighteenth century is an unexplained mystery of the Garfield writing personality. It could be that it allows release from the realistic inhibitions that increasingly gathered round the novel from mid-Victorian times onwards. Garfield's is a lawless world; or, more precisely, a world in which the rule of law is itself a contender, is trying to assert itself but is not to be relied on for protection. Men are greatly dependent on their own quickness of hand, of foot, of eye, of wit. The world is one in which great and small rogues are forever busy and the Devil is there to take the hindmost. The author seems steeped in his period; even when writing in the third person he commonly puts 'mistook' or 'forsook' or 'forgot' for 'mistaken' or 'forsaken' or 'forgotten', and he will write 'twenty pound' rather than 'twenty pounds'. But this is not the eighteenth century that might be reconstructed by an historical novelist. It is original, organic, springing straight from the Garfield imagination; though I believe that the work of other writers, and artists, has provided an essential compost. You may well discern something of Stevenson in Garfield's first book, *Jack Holborn* (1964), and something of Dickens everywhere. You may be sure that Garfield knows the work of Fielding and Hogarth, among much else from the eighteenth century itself. There are less obvious writers whose work can fruitfully be considered in relation to his: the great Russian novelists, especially Dostoievsky; even Jane Austen; even Emily Brontë. A rich literary soil is not simply constituted.

The first novel, *Jack Holborn*, showed many of its author's qualities already strongly developed, and immediately appeared remarkable when it first came out. In comparison with later books it has several weaknesses. On the surface it is a tale of piracy, murder, treasure, treachery, shipwreck and ultimate fortune, all in the best tradition of the sea adventure story. And so it will be read by children and by most other readers. There are also two separate questions of identity. One is simple: just who *is* the hero-narrator, the foundling Jack Holborn, so named from the parish in which he was abandoned? The other is disconcerting: how can it be that identical faces cover such different personalities as those of the distinguished Judge and the wicked pirate captain? Confusion between real and apparent good and evil is a recurrent Garfield theme; but the device used in *Jack Holborn* – the introduction of identical twins of opposite character – is crude in comparison with, for instance, the moral complexity of *The Drummer Boy* five years later. And *Jack Holborn* has other flaws. The story, of which the first three quarters are gripping, falls away in the final quarter; the narrator is brave, generous and well-meaning, but he is not interesting. Yet the Garfield style and vision are already unmistakable, and although the writing is not yet fully ablaze with metaphor in the later Garfield manner it rises at times to a staccato poetry.

Devil-in-the-Fog (1966), the second novel, again revolves at length around questions of identity. The narrator George Treet, from being a member of a family of travelling players, is translated suddenly to the position of heir apparent to Sir John Dexter, baronet. In the misty grounds of the great house lurks Sir John's unloving brother, newly cut out of the succession. But who is the true villain, and is George really gentleman or player? The book shows one clear advance on *Jack Holborn*: the difficulty of making the narrator into an effective character in his own right is overcome. The artless George, in telling his story, allows us to see more of him than he can see of himself; we perceive, for instance, the honest vulgarity that makes him unacceptable to Sir John as an heir. And here enters another Garfield theme, that of true and false feeling; for we can contrast and appraise at their proper values the simple vanity of the Treets and the chilly pride of Sir John. But the story, although straightforward in theme and feeling, is complicated in terms of actual incident; and not even the Garfield energy is quite enough to drive it successfully through its own convolutions and lengthy denouement. Although it deservedly won the first *Guardian* award for children's fiction, *Devil-in-the-Fog* still seems to me to display outstanding promise rather than outstanding achievement.

Smith (1967), the first of Leon Garfield's third-person narrations, was a stronger and more straightforward story than either of its predecessors. The hero Smith—he doesn't seem to have any Christian name—is a twelve-year-old pickpocket who

> was a sooty spirit of the violent and ramshackle town, and inhabited the tumbledown mazes about fat St Paul's like the subtle air itself. A rat was a snail beside Smith, and the most his thousand victims ever got of him was the powerful whiff of his passing and a cold draught in their dexterously emptied pockets.

Two moments of pity—for a dying man and for a blind magistrate—get Smith caught up in a whirl of villainy, and set him perilously at odds with a world of thieves, highwaymen, murderers. Over this world loom Newgate Gaol and the gallows. Its music is the Tyburn Carol:

> Five yards of rope,
> Four sextons digging,
> Three parsons praying,
> Two horses drawing,
> And a felon in an elm-tree.

Through it move, side by side, the small, sharp, devious Smith and the upright tragic figure of the blind magistrate; by them wickedness is unmasked and a fortune regained. And the figures of Smith and the magistrate, apparent opposites, are meanwhile moving towards each other, impelled by a growing respect and understanding. Once more there is a puzzle of identity: who is the mysterious Mr Black, and what has become of the long-departed son of the murdered man? There is also the confusion of good and evil; for the respectable young attorney who is paying his attentions to the magistrate's daughter is not what he seems, while it is the third-rate highwayman Lord Tom who saves the sum of things at the cost of his own life. In *Smith*, it seems to me that the forward progress of the story is no longer hindered by entanglement in complications; it knows where it is going and drives steadily towards its powerful climax. It is more unified, more of a novel than its two predecessors or its successor; it is not Garfield's richest book but it is the most obviously successful of his first four.

Black Jack (1968) is a more complex book than *Smith*, and, in its beginning and end, more powerful. It is however less satisfactory in structure. Black Jack is 'a vast ruffian, nearly seven foot high and broad to match, who'd terrorized the lanes about Knightsbridge till a quart of rum and five police officers laid him low'. A silver tube inserted in his throat cheats the hangman, and cheats the 'Tyburn widow', Mrs Gorgandy, dealer in corpses; for, by the time she's arranged a sale of the body, there's no body to sell. Black Jack is out and about in the reluctant company of young Tolly, draper's apprentice and hero of the story.

But now in the middle third of the book Black Jack withdraws to the wings; the centre of the stage is taken by the love story of Tolly and the young girl from the madhouse, Belle, who travel the lanes together with the well-meaning fairground quack Dr Carmody. Only in the apocalyptic closing chapters – set in London at the time of the great earthquake scare of 1750 – does the giant, chastened in spirit but in full strength of body, come into his own. For, as tremors shake London and the Northern Lights spread across the sky, and the end of the world is declared to be at hand, it is Black Jack who breaks open the madhouse and helps Belle and Tolly to find their happiness. The love story here is fresh and touching. But the structure is perhaps more like that of a symphony – one with powerful opening and closing movements and quieter ones in between – than that of a novel, in which one might wish for a more continuous progress, a build-up of tension towards the climax.

Garfield's latest novel so far, *The Drummer Boy* (1970), is the most ambitious of all and the most complex in ideas and feeling although not in plot. Its hero Charlie Samson is everyone's golden lad, the embodiment of all unfulfilled dreams and lost ideals. With Charlie the story moves from the field of battle, in which ten thousand scarlet soldiers have been mown down, to London, where the responsible General is trying to save his skin. In thrall to the General's beautiful and apparently dying daughter Sophia, Charlie is ready to perjure himself and shift the General's guilt to a haunted wretch of a scapegoat. He is brought to his senses by the cowardly, fat, pansy surgeon Mister Shaw and the common servant-girl Charity.

Clearly the book is concerned with the evils of false

romanticism. The brief and doubtful glory of the battlefield is a poor exchange for the slow ripening of a lifetime which we see awaiting Charlie in the story's happy ending. The brief and doubtful glory of serving belle-dame-sans-merci Sophia and her exalted, hollow father is nothing in comparison with the warmth of an honest wench with twenty pounds in the bank and a loving nature. Again there is the bewildering interchange of good and evil; for the apparently natural love of Charlie for Sophia turns out to be a deadly menace, while the seemingly unnatural love of Mister Shaw for Charlie, though it is hopeless, pathetic, incapable of fruition, is beneficent. It would be possible to see Mister Shaw as the ambiguous hero of this story: himself the battlefield, with his healing gift at war with half a dozen ignoble purposes. Charlie as hero is so much a receptacle for the hopes and dreams of others that in himself he is an empty vessel. But at last he loses his drum, the symbol of his virginity of mind and body, and returns with Charity on his arm to the New Forest where he began. The real story of Charlie Samson starts where the book leaves off.

I do not think *The Drummer Boy* is quite the major triumph that Garfield has been promising ever since *Jack Holborn*, but I am sure it will come. In the meantime, he has one small but perfect work to his credit in *Mister Corbett's Ghost*, which was published in England in 1969 as part of a triptych with two other stories. It is the tale of an apothecary's apprentice, Benjamin, who wishes his harsh master dead, and on New Year's Eve finds an old man who can grant the wish, at a price. But the ghost of Mister Corbett lingers with Benjamin and is more pitiable, more human even, than Mister Corbett was in life; and the boy is happy, in the end, to undo his bargain. Whether this is a story of the supernatural or an externalizing of inner processes is a matter of interpretation, or perhaps of the reader's own development. The themes are those of responsibility for one's actions and of the dreadful destructiveness of revenge; and in his dealings with Mister Corbett as corpse and then as ghost Benjamin goes through the stages of guilt: fear, shame, remorse, compassion. This is a tale told with total command; its temperature goes down, down, far below zero before returning all the more effectively to the warmth of living flesh. I would say, and not lightly, that it can be compared to *A Christmas Carol*.

Leon Garfield

The most obvious characteristic of Leon Garfield I have left until the end. He treats the English language with a mastery that sometimes verges on outrage. Effortlessly, page after page and line after line, he creates his individual and vivid images. 'He jerked the candle down, thereby causing banisters and certain pieces of respectable mahogany furniture to take fright and crouch in their own shadows.' I take this almost at random from *Mister Corbett's Ghost*, still open after consultation for the previous paragraph. And, in the same story, as the New Year is let in at the Spaniards' Inn: '"Hands, gents! Hands must be joined!" shouted the landlord, and stretched out his portly arms like a well-fed signpost.' Garfield's metaphors tend to be strongly visual. But he does not only see; he touches, tastes and smells. (An analysis of the smells in his novels might be curiously illuminating.) As a man with medical knowledge he is well aware of the perishable human body, the too too solid, or sullied, flesh. In treating of life as it comes, more rough than smooth, he is not unduly fastidious. Yet he can be gentle, as in the love of Belle and Tolly in *Black Jack*. There is a remarkable passage of dialogue which begins when Belle says to Tolly:

> 'Tell me about the sea.'
> 'Water, Belle, as far as the eye can see.'
> 'What noise does it make?'
> 'It sighs and whispers and slaps and sometimes roars.'
> 'What is it like when the wind blows?'
> 'Huge and terrible. It rises up in dark, shiny walls, all foamy on top. Then down it crashes and the beach stones fly.'
> 'What is it like when the sun shines?'
> 'Like a great looking-glass, Belle. Very smooth and bright and still-looking.'
> 'What's under the sea, Tolly?'
> 'Green darkness—like a great forest. Strange flowers and weeds and fish and sunken ships and treasures . . .'

This is poetry; indeed, it is love poetry, full of innocent sensuality. It surprises, but it does not surprise too much, for Leon Garfield can do anything with words and his touch is very sure. And that last sentence, about the things that lie beneath the sea, brings me back in closing to the phrase from 'Full fathom five' which seems best to describe his talent: rich and strange. I do not believe in singling out a writer as 'the best'; books and their authors are only to a limited extent comparable, and should not be seen as competing against each other. But I have livelier expectations from Leon Garfield than from anyone else whose work is being published on a children's list in England today.

Leon Garfield writes:

The beginnings are hard to remember. I always wanted to write. I do recall soggy stories à la Tolstoy . . . weird tales à la Poe . . . and then drifting towards farcical thrillers. Then to Lewis-Carroll-like efforts, then to Hans Andersen . . . It all seems to have been rather like a pendulum – swinging and scratching wildly from side to side till at last it settled somewhere in the middle. I seemed to drift to writing for children; or rather, I drifted to the sort of writing I like – which can have wildly exciting adventures *and* something of character and morality.

Really, what I try to write is that old-fashioned thing the family novel, accessible to the twelve-year-old and readable by his elders.

I use the quest for identity, which seems to occur pretty often, because I have a passion for secrets and mystery. And the secret and mystery of another individual seems to me the only mystery one can unravel endlessly – and still be uncertain. As for good and evil: I suppose I use large moral issues (in which I feel justified in taking sides) as a sort of skeleton of the work: something to which I can relate varied incidents and thus give them a certain unity. I *think* I do this by making my central character aware of the issue embedded in the incident. But of course if it doesn't fit it has to go – perhaps to be used again elsewhere.

Colourful incidents have been rather lacking in my life. My war service was distinguished by a steady adherence to the rank of private in the Medical Corps. Yet those marvellously boring five years did have moments on which I've drawn repeatedly: incidents in my brief period of 'war crimes investigation'; incidents comic and bloody in the work of a busy hospital . . .

I suppose my earlier writings were invariably based on literary experience. But from *Jack Holborn* onward I used direct experience, however much transcribed. For my African jungle, I remember, I went several times to Kew Gardens and Epping Forest. For my seafaring I went once to Jersey and a dozen times to Greenwich. Just so long as I had something to go on—something to remember, as it were—I was all right.

Leon Garfield

Bibliography

JACK HOLBORN. Longman, 1964; Pantheon, 1965.

DEVIL-IN-THE-FOG. Longman, 1966; Pantheon, 1966.

SMITH. Longman, 1967; Pantheon, 1967.

BLACK JACK. Longman, 1968; Pantheon, 1969.

MISTER CORBETT'S GHOST. Pantheon, 1968.

THE BOY AND THE MONKEY. Heinemann, 1969; Franklin Watts, 1970.

MISTER CORBETT'S GHOST, AND OTHER STORIES. Longman, 1969. (Contains *Mister Corbett's Ghost, Vaarlem and Tripp* and *The Simpleton.*)

THE RESTLESS GHOST: THREE STORIES. Pantheon, 1969. (Contains *The Restless Ghost, Vaarlem and Tripp* and *The Simpleton.*)

THE DRUMMER BOY. Longman, 1970; Pantheon, 1970.

THE GOD BENEATH THE SEA (with Edward Blishen). Longman, 1970; Pantheon, 1971.

THE CAPTAIN'S WATCH. Heinemann, 1971.

THE STRANGE AFFAIR OF ADELAIDE HARRIS. Longman, 1971; Pantheon, 1971.

Short stories by Leon Garfield include *The Questioners* in WINTER'S TALES FOR CHILDREN 4, edited by M. R. Hodgkin (Macmillan, 1968) and the title story in THE RESTLESS GHOST AND OTHER ENCOUNTERS AND EXPERIENCES, edited by Susan Dickinson (Collins, 1970). A play, *The Cabbage and the Rose,* written with Patrick Hardy, was published in MISCELLANY FOUR, edited by Edward Blishen (Oxford University Press, 1967).

Alan Garner

Alan Garner was born in 1935 and educated at Alderley Edge Primary School, Manchester Grammar School, and Magdalen College, Oxford. He was a keen athlete at school and won many championships for his county as a sprinter. He left Oxford to become a full-time writer, and now lives with his three children in an ancient cottage in Cheshire. His principal books are The Weirdstone of Brisingamen *(1960)*, The Moon of Gomrath *(1963)*, Elidor *(1965) and* The Owl Service *(1967).*

Alan Garner is, at present, the most discussed contemporary British writer for children. He is also one of the few who are known to some extent among adults outside the literary world. All short-lists of leading children's authors include his name; a name to which the adjective 'brilliant' has a growing tendency to attach itself.

This reputation has not been achieved by high output. Between 1960 and 1967 he published the four novels discussed here, and some minor work, including a children's nativity play, *Holly from the Bongs*. At the time of writing, his fifth novel has been awaited for nearly three years. But his books, though few, have had an extraordinarily powerful impact; they have been felt and not forgotten.

All his books can be broadly – very broadly – described as fantasies. All are based to a great extent on old legend and story. A full-scale study of Garner's work would call for much research among Celtic, Scandinavian and other mythology and in widespread fields of folklore, anthropology, history and prehistory. I have not the space here for any such study, nor am I qualified to produce one. And this may not be entirely a disadvantage. Although a scholarly approach would have its interest, I am not at all sure that the detailed exploration of sources is required or even desirable before attempting a brief critical assessment. For an author is only entitled, and would only wish, to take credit for his sources to the extent to which he has absorbed them and incorporated them effectively into his own work. And when he has done so they are not 'sources' any more; they are part of himself.

Because Garner's four novels came out at intervals of two and three years, they show their differences – and the author's development – more clearly than do the works of more prolific writers. Alan Garner has never stood still. His stories have become less complicated but more complex, less crowded but more intricately ramified. Action has become less crude but more significant. The later books are finer. Admittedly, even fineness has its price. *The Weirdstone of Brisingamen* (1960) was Garner's first book; it is complicated, crowded, full of crude action; and of its kind it still seems to me to be excellent. Its author was hard on himself when he described it as 'a fairly bad book'. *The Owl Service* (1967) is complex and intricate, its action more restrained and much more meaningful. It has not the same brute vitality. But although an overall comparison between two such different books is hardly possible, it seems fair to say that *The Owl Service* is by far the more notable achievement.

When *The Weirdstone of Brisingamen* first appeared, it was widely hinted that Garner was indebted to J. R. R. Tolkien. In fact he did not then know Tolkien's work. The great difference between Tolkien and early Garner is that Tolkien creates a world of magic apart from our own while Garner brings magic into our own world, here and now. This is an important principle with him. 'If we are in Eldorado,' he wrote in a *New Statesman* review, 'and we find a mandrake, then OK, so it's a mandrake: in Eldorado anything goes. But, by force of imagination compel the reader to believe that there is a mandrake in a garden in Mayfield Road, Ulverston, Lancs, then when you pull up that mandrake it is really going to scream; and possibly the reader will, too.'

Garner's magic is at once enhanced and made more credible by the solidity of his settings. In *The Weirdstone of Brisingamen*, and its sequel *The Moon of Gomrath* (1963), the background is the Cheshire countryside around Alderley Edge: firm, hard, topographically accurate. It is so plainly authentic that it gives the illusion of authenticating the story.

The first book has a strong, straightforward plot. Two children, Colin and Susan, find they are in possession of the magic stone that guards the company of knights who will one day wake to save the world. They lose the stone to evil forces, recover it, and make a perilous dash across country to put it in the hands of the good magician Cadellin. (The story is, of course, a pendant to existing legend, and Cadellin is known by other names.) On each side new ranks of creatures are called successively into the struggle: dwarfs, goblins, warlocks, scarecrows, a lady of the lake, a fairy horse, pin-headed troll-women. Sometimes one has the impression that ever more properties are being brought out of a bottomless wardrobe; at other times it seems as if a game of high-speed chess is going on. There is not much subtlety, but the cliffhanging excitement is intense and not even Garner has surpassed it.

In *The Moon of Gomrath*, which appeared three years later, the story-line is weaker although this is more obvious from analysis afterwards than while the book is being read. But the imaginative power and the poetry with which Garner invests his traditional materials are immensely increased.

The surface action breaks into two parts. In the first, Susan is possessed by an ancient, formless mischief called the Brollachan, and to free her Colin must find and pluck a magic flower; in the second, Colin is held prisoner by a vengeful witch, the Morrigan, and eventually rescued. But there is much more to it than that. The Brollachan, if I understand matters correctly, is a manifestation of the Old Evil, against which the cerebral High Magic of Cadellin is too delicate a weapon. There is nothing for it but to call in the Old Magic: a fierce, elemental magic of sun and moon, earth and blood, surviving from crueller times. It is the Old Magic that draws Colin by moonlight along the old straight track to find the vital flower. The High Magic of thoughts and spells has held the Old Magic in check, but now it has been disturbed; and under the moon of Gomrath, when the Old Magic sleeps most lightly, the children are instrumental in releasing it. And although in the end the Old Evil is defeated, the Old Magic rides dangerously free.

It will be seen that magic has taken successive forms which

parallel the growth of civilization. More than that, there are levels of existence other than our own: 'the darkness and unformed life that is called Abred by wizards' and 'the Threshold of the Summer Stars, as far beyond this world as Abred is below'. In *The Moon of Gomrath* the poetry and potency of magic are matched. There is a crucial moment in which the children, bringing fire to an ancient mound on the Eve of Gomrath, arouse three warrior-horsemen: at first unstable as pictures in flame, but becoming solid, real and terrible.

> They were dressed all in red: red were their tunics, and red their cloaks; red their eyes, and red their long manes of hair bound back with circlets of red gold; three red shields on their backs, and three red spears in their hands; three red horses under them, and red was the harness. Red were they all, weapons and clothing and hair, both horses and men.

This is the Wild Hunt; and in the way it is let loose there seems to be a suggestion of the loosing of wild fire. Yet the power of the Old Magic is associated, above all, with moonlight. By moonlight Colin seeks and finds the magic flower; by moonlight the Wild Hunt is aroused; Colin's imprisonment is in a ruined house that by moonlight alone becomes whole.

Both in *The Weirdstone of Brisingamen* and *The Moon of Gomrath*, the human element pales beside the magic one. As characters, Colin and Susan are hardly even sketched in the former book, and although they emerge more positively in *The Moon of Gomrath*, they still lack individuality: basically they are just 'a boy' and 'a girl'. This is not to my mind a major weakness. You cannot do everything in the same book. Rapid action and the evocation of breathtaking magical worlds are not easily reconciled with the quieter, slower-paced unfolding of character; there may even be a case, in stories like these, for leaving the human participants as blank spaces into which readers can insert themselves. At the end of *The Moon of Gomrath*, Garner appeared to leave the way open for a third book with the same characters and setting; but he has not written one, perhaps feeling that the possibilities in that direction were limited.

His third novel, *Elidor*, was totally different. For the first time, the magical country is separated from the everyday world. Elidor's position in time and space is a question of metaphysics rather than of cosmology, for acts in one world can be reflected in the other. Four children, exploring a slum clearance area in the back streets of Manchester, find themselves translated to the once green, now blighted, land of Elidor. Their rôle there is to fulfil the ancient prophecy of the Starved Fool and restore light and life to the land. After a brief visit, shadowed by menace, they return to Manchester, bringing with them for safe-keeping the Treasures of Elidor, in which its life partly resides. Roland has a spear, David a sword, Nicholas a golden stone, Helen a pearl-rimmed bowl. In the daily world the Treasures become mere bits of junk—except that they have disconcerting effects on electrical equipment. The children bury them in their suburban garden; and now the interactions of our world and Elidor intensify until the spectacular climax in which a unicorn gallops through slum streets, and the Song of Findhorn is heard, and a sunburst sweeps Elidor with colour as the horned beast dies with its head in Helen's lap.

The sources of *Elidor*, the ideas that went into it, are many. If there is one special key, I am fairly sure it lies in Jessie Weston's book *From Ritual to Romance*, which links the Golden Bough with the Grail legend, and is further linked in *Elidor* with the myth of the unicorn. The waste land of Elidor is the waste land which gives T. S. Eliot's poem its title. It is the male procreative act that renews life and that takes place in the dying Song of Findhorn; it is no mere incidental detail that Helen's treasure is the bowl—or grail—and that it breaks when the unicorn lays its head in her lap.

Few readers, and probably no child, will recognize the underlying material; nor is it particularly important either to them or to a brief appraisal of the book. The question is whether it has been absorbed; whether, unknown to the reader, its power has come through and is now Garner's. It seems to me that it has, and that the ending of *Elidor* has a splendour which is totally intrinsic. But I do not think the book as a whole is fully successful, and the trouble lies in the land of Elidor itself. After the children's initial visit we see practically nothing of it; we do not know what is going on. There are hints that evil is at work, but what evil we never learn. The trouble may be that nothing really *can* happen there; it is the waste land, the dead land waiting for life. Whatever the explanation, it is frustrating that a magical country is created and then abandoned early in the proceedings.

But the fact that two thirds of the story takes place in suburban Manchester in conditions of everyday life means that there is more scope here than in Garner's two earlier novels for the development of human character. I think in this case it is a valid criticism that very little such development takes place. Of the four children, Roland, the youngest ('Childe Rowland to the Dark Tower came'), has the greatest power to act in both worlds at once; has the greatest understanding, takes all the important initiatives; has indeed a spirit and doggedness that make him flesh and blood. Helen plays a special part, but it is purely functional; as an individual she is a cipher. The two older boys are indistinguishable, and the parents are stock figures of the suburban commuter belt. The children are ill matched to the story on another scale, too. As Elidor's saviours they have been the subjects of prophecy there; their likenesses appear in an old and treasured book 'written so long ago that we have only legend to tell us about it'. To create four apparently ordinary suburban children who would be equal to a rôle of the importance that this implies would be very difficult. Garner has not done it.

And so to *The Owl Service*, a book that again breaks fresh ground and to my mind has a new maturity and authority: a book written by a man who has mastered his craft and knows just what he is about. I would say that *The Owl Service* is – against formidable competition – the most remarkable single novel to appear on a children's list in the 1960s. But, as is the way with highly-ranked books for children, it has come in for a great deal of uncritical praise. Adulation is not my purpose here.

The theme is characteristic of Garner: the irruption of old legend into modern life. The difference lies in the deepening and strengthening of the human element of the story, and in the grasp of the emotional truth of a situation existing here and now. In Garner's earlier books the people were little more than pawns: the power lay in external forces. In *The Owl Service*, the legend and its re-enactments are in their true place as phenomena arising out of the nature of humanity rather than working on it from outside. People – unthinking, vulnerable, little knowing what harm they can do to themselves and others – carry the potentiality for disaster within them. They also carry within them the potentiality for avoiding disaster.

The legend behind and within *The Owl Service* is the story from the Fourth Branch of the Mabinogion which tells how the magician Gwydion made a wife of flowers for Lleu Llaw Gyffes, and how the wife betrayed her husband and took Gronw Pebyr for her lover. Gronw was killed by Lleu, and, in punishment for the wife's sin, Gwydion turned her into Blodeuwydd, the owl, to which even other birds are hostile.

Garner's novel is set in a valley supposed to be the same setting as that of the old story, in which we learn that the agony of Blodeuwydd builds up from time to time over the years and forces its way out afresh in similar, recurrent situations. And now, in the big house, are Alison and Roger, young English people who have been made stepbrother and stepsister by the marriage of Alison's mother to Roger's father; and, mixing uneasily with them on Christian-name terms of not-quite-equality, is Gwyn, the housekeeper's son, the Welsh grammar-school boy with a huge chip on his shoulder. With these three the vicious triangle re-forms; the power of Blodeuwydd – 'she wants to be flowers, but you make her owls' – grows, throbs nearer, builds to unbearable tension, and comes to wild release in the last few pages. Disaster is at hand. When the drama was last enacted, a generation ago, it ended with death. This time the worst is averted; and it is averted by insensitive, unimaginative English Roger, and not by the passionate, intelligent Welsh boy Gwyn – the few necessary words of forgiveness and understanding are more than the tortured Gwyn can spare.

The supernatural is used sparingly, although with great effect. *The Owl Service* is, as I have suggested, essentially a human story, and I do not doubt that if he had been so minded Garner could have done without any element of fantasy at all. The memory of the legend, the knowledge that this valley was its setting and that the tragedy had recurred here more than once, a sense of impending and barely-escapable doom: these might well have sufficed. This is not to say that the author should have *made* them suffice. A man must write his books in his own way.

Among the themes of *The Owl Service* is that of relationships between the generations, and, specifically, the damage that possessive parents can do to their children. Another is that of 'Welsh and English', with all that the words connote. Gwyn and his embittered mother Nancy are of the 'inferior' race, the occupied country, whereas Alison and Roger and their parents are of the one-time ascendancy. And there is a class distinction of some nicety between Alison and her mother on the one hand and Roger and his father on the other; for the latter two are not quite out of the top drawer. The dialogue is subtle, quick, accurate, full of nuances, and is a great advance on Garner's previous work. The characterization at individual level is still a little patchy. To me, it seems that Gwyn and his mother Nancy are excellent, that Roger's father Clive is a well-drawn major-minor character, and that Alison's mother, Margaret, is outlined with remarkable clarity considering that she never actually appears. But Alison and Roger have a total ordinariness which, however deliberate, leaves them, like the children in *Elidor*, unequal to the demands of their part in the story. They are not strong enough, not positive enough, to make two corners of this eternal and passionate triangle.

This last point is made at some length by Eleanor Cameron in an essay on *The Owl Service* in the *Wilson Library Bulletin* for December, 1969. Miss Cameron goes so far as to suggest that Garner has 'debilitated' his material by choosing immature teenagers as the members of his triangle. I think, however, that Miss Cameron, although often perceptive, is unduly severe in her conclusions about *The Owl Service*. It surprises me considerably that she finds in it a lack of 'passion and power and force from the depths'. I would say exactly the opposite: that these are the qualities which the book most conspicuously possesses.

The Owl Service is not, in fact, an easy novel to discuss. It has a haunting, elusive quality which makes it hard to feel sure that one has it in one's critical grip. There is a disturbing sense that the book as it stands is not the whole story, that behind each incident that is fixed in words there lies something shifting and ambiguous, something that can be felt but not expressed.

Garner's next move is unknown as I write. I feel it must again be in a new direction. He will not repeat his successes, or even seek new successes at the same level as before, and this means that he cannot publish lightly. It is not even certain that he will continue to work in the novel form. But his potentiality is very great, and he is always likely to do something one would not have guessed at until it was there. It would only be surprising if he ceased to surprise us.

Invited to look back, and ahead, from 1970, when he had been a published author for ten years, Alan Garner wrote:

To try to assess a decade of being published, and to look forwards, is an uncomfortable and invidious job, and may be pointless. It's certainly hard – like trying to see the back of one's own head.

The decade has been fourteen years long, because a book had to be written first, and then sold. There were seven years of unrelieved poverty, four of breadline subsistence, and the last three have been acceptable, a little above the national average. But there were few times when the situation felt desperate: it's been much easier to start from zero than it would have been to have reduced an accustomed standard of living.

Prime factors become clear within days. It is helpful to eat, to be warm, to be dry. Anything beyond is a luxury, whether it's a plank to sleep on or an ocean-going yacht.

There are no complaints about the fact of poverty, but the public attitude towards the intending professional can be searing. To write a good book is one of the great skills, calling for as much application and ability as a First Class Honours Degree. We, through the Government, think little of supporting a young man at Oxford to read Homer, so that he can join the ranks of Shell and Unilever, but we expect the professional artist to practise as an amateur, after 'work'. I reckoned that by my leaving Oxford, giving up my various grants, and applying for National Assistance, the Government was saving about £50 a year while I was writing my first book. The logic is simple; naïve in practice.

The book was published, and a critical success, which had little effect on my pocket. My publisher told me at the start that, if we both applied ourselves, it would be about ten years before I could expect the books to look after me. In the event, it was seven years.

I've dwelt on the economics because they are important, and have dominated the background of existence. They have never directly affected the work. So what of that work? What has been achieved? In my own terms, enough to justify the activity. One quite good poem; one good book (*The Owl Service*); one complete success (the text of *Holly from the Bongs*); one good short story (*Feel Free*); one statement of prose where the words acted with total precision (the last paragraph of Chapter 26 of *The Owl Service*). It's a fair harvest.

The future is unpredictable. I have never thought of myself as a writer. I function; words were what I could use best at the start, that's all. The printed word is still an insoluble challenge, but it is only one form of expression. Film, paint, music, shape, speech all have their advantages, and are waiting to be used. My only ambition is to do something well.

Alan Garner

Bibliography

THE WEIRDSTONE OF BRISINGAMEN. Collins, 1960; Walck, 1969.
THE MOON OF GOMRATH. Collins, 1963; Walck, 1967.
ELIDOR. Collins, 1965; Walck, 1967.
HOLLY FROM THE BONGS (with Roger Hill). Collins, 1966.
THE OLD MAN OF MOW. Collins, 1967.
THE OWL SERVICE. Collins, 1967; Walck, 1968.

Alan Garner edited THE HAMISH HAMILTON BOOK OF GOBLINS (Hamish Hamilton, 1969; Walck, 1969, as A CAVALCADE OF GOBLINS) and his short stories for children include *Galgoid the Hewer* in WINTER'S TALES FOR CHILDREN 2, edited by Caroline Hillier (Macmillan, London, 1966) and *Feel Free* in THE RESTLESS GHOST AND OTHER ENCOUNTERS AND EXPERIENCES, edited by Susan Dickinson (Collins, 1970).

Madeleine L'Engle

Madeleine L'Engle was born in New York City, the daughter of Charles Wadsworth Camp, author and playwright. She went to school in the United States and Switzerland, and graduated with honours from Smith College. During a brief stint in the theatre she met her actor husband Hugh Franklin; says that she 'met him in The Cherry Orchard *and married him in* The Joyous Season'. *They kept a small-town general store in Connecticut for six years before returning to New York, where they still live. They have three children and are now grandparents. Miss L'Engle's novels for children and young people include* Meet the Austins *(1960),* A Wrinkle in Time *(1962), which won the Newbery Medal, and* The Young Unicorns *(1968).*

Madeleine L'Engle is a curiously-gifted, curiously-learned, curiously-imperfect writer. Her novels for young people seem to me to be full of contradictions. They are so often exciting and stylishly written, yet so often complicated beyond endurance or unintentionally comic or embarrassing, that I find them harder to assess than those of almost anyone else.

Miss L'Engle's main themes are the clash of good and evil, the difficulty and necessity of deciding which is which and of committing oneself, the search for fulfilment and self-knowledge. These themes are determined by what the author *is*; and she is a practising and active Christian. Many writers' religious beliefs appear immaterial to their work; Miss L'Engle's are crucial. She is a thoughtful, highly intelligent, questioning Christian, and this means that, to her, the Christian faith is no simple affair but a mystery beyond human understanding. She well knows that she does not have, any more than Milton or any orthodox Christian writer ever since, the answers to the great and perennial problems. If God is good and all-powerful, why does evil exist? If God has foreknowledge, how can man have free will? Why does God not manifest himself? Where 'is' he, where 'are' heaven and hell? Miss L'Engle, I believe, sees clearly enough that the only possible answer to all these questions is, 'We do not know; we are not equipped to know.' As Uncle Douglas tells Vicky Austin in *The Moon By Night*:

> 'If there is a God, he's infinite and we're finite, and therefore we can't ever understand him. The minute anybody starts telling you what God thinks, or exactly why he does such and such, beware . . . When I wasn't much older than you I decided that God, a kind and loving God, could never be proved. In fact there are, as you've been seeing lately, a lot of arguments against him. But there isn't any point to life without him. Without him we're just a skin disease on the face of the earth, and I feel too strongly about the human spirit to be able to settle for that. So what I did for a long time was to live life *as though* I believed in God. And eventually I found that *as though* had turned into reality.'

But Miss L'Engle has her certainties. The chief one, and clearly to her the chief commandment, is that we are to love one another. And a key centre of goodness on earth is, or is symbolized in, the life of a loving family.

> I think the closest we ever come in this naughty world to realizing unity in diversity is round a family table. I felt it at their (the Austins') table, the wholeness of the family unit, freely able to expand to include friends . . . and yet each person in that unit complete, individual, unique, valued.

That is Canon Tallis in *The Young Unicorns*. Clearly both he and Uncle Douglas are expressing views with which the author is sympathetic.

So the Austin family, who are leading participants in three novels and have spiritual cousins in two more (the Murrys in *A Wrinkle in Time* and the O'Keefes in *The Arm of the Starfish*), are not merely characters; they are representatives of the kind of good to which in this imperfect world we can aspire. And perhaps they are a little too good to be true.

Two books, *Meet the Austins* (1960) and *The Moon By Night*

(1963), are about the family life of the Austins, and are told in the first person by daughter Vicky, a young teenager. *Meet the Austins* is episodic, has no single story-line, and shows more than anything else the family reactions to a series of situations. *The Moon By Night* is the story of a coast-to-coast camping trip which is also a voyage of self-discovery for Vicky. The family is solid, warm and loving. Dr Austin – it is significant, I am sure, that he is a healer – is an almost Godlike figure: kind but sometimes stern, authoritative, always knowing what needs to be done and able to do it. Mother is talented yet willing to give all to the family; and is as nearly perfect a mother as Dr Austin is a father. John is the ideal elder brother: handsome, protective, resourceful, and improbably patient and understanding with the younger ones. Rob, the smallest, is bright and sweet and well-behaved; it is interesting that he is again and again referred to as a little boy and is always seen from a higher eye-level than his own. The girls are more human: Vicky has stirrings of adolescent restlessness, and younger sister Suzy even has plain ordinary faults. But then there are Uncle Douglas, and Aunt Elena, and Grandfather, who is a retired minister; and all three again seem to me to be a little too good. Not only that; I sense a certain smugness in the Austins. They *know* how nice and how cultured they are, and they appreciate themselves. Here are John and Vicky talking:

> 'Mother says she can never stay mad at Daddy, no matter how hard she tries. And Daddy says, "*Stay* mad! You won't even let me *get* mad at you," and then they laugh. Aren't you sorry for people who don't laugh, Vicky?'
> 'Yes. And people who don't love music and books.'
> 'And people,' John said.

The references to music and books are very much to the point. Artistic talent is present or latent in several members of the family, and the Austins attract talented friends. Singing is traditional with them, and when, in *The Young Unicorns*, Canon Tallis comes to dinner, they sing the Tallis canon in his honour, as a round, for grace. Why not? It would be a natural and charming gesture in such a family; and yet I must confess to a slight acidity in my reaction: Yes, they *would*.

Life in the Austin family is not entirely relaxed. Vicky, in both *Meet the Austins* and *The Moon By Night* seems to suffer undue guilt for very minor failings. Dr Austin sometimes lectures her without apology:

> 'Vicky, I can just see you thinking, "Mother and Daddy are sermonising again." Well, we're going to go on preaching, and,' Daddy's voice grew more serious, 'I expect you to listen.'

And both Dr Austin and squarish elder brother John are distinctly stuffy when advances are made to Vicky by a cynical – but really quite harmless – boy called Zachary in *The Moon By Night*. Maybe it is just the result of a sense of inferiority in one who perceives himself to be neither as nice nor as cultured as the Austins, but I am afraid I cannot like them as much as the author does.

Madeleine L'Engle's novels do not confine themselves to family life, however. Her other aspect, as a writer for children and young people, is a remarkably different one. She is the author of – so far – three rapid-action adventure stories: *A Wrinkle in Time* (1962), *The Arm of the Starfish* (1966), and *The Young Unicorns* (1968.) All three are to some extent science-based, and, indeed, *A Wrinkle in Time* is usually described as science-fiction. Miss L'Engle will clearly have no truck with any notion that science is either unfeminine or inimical to religion. In *A Wrinkle in Time*, the heroine's father is a scientist who has been experimenting with a means of short-circuiting time (necessary if vast distances in space are to be covered). In *The Arm of the Starfish*, experiments of a marine biologist which could have profound implications for people are the mainspring of the plot, while a means of control for the laser-beam plays an important part in *The Young Unicorns*.

The contrast between the family stories and the others is by no means complete, however. In the three action-novels, the L'Engle of the Austin books is still there. In fact, in *The Young Unicorns*, the Austins themselves are there, having moved from their quiet New England town to New York City. In these three books family relationships are found as a core of warmth and reassurance in baffling and dangerous situations. And the preoccupation with good and evil runs strongly through them all.

In *A Wrinkle in Time*, the clash of good and evil is at cosmic level. Much of the action is concerned with the rescue by the heroine Meg and her friend Calvin O'Keefe of Meg's father and brother, prisoners of a great brain called IT which controls the lives of a zombie population on a planet called Camazotz. Here evil is obviously the reduction of people to a mindless mass, while good is individuality, art and love. It is the sheer power of love which enables Meg to triumph over IT, for love is the force that she has and that IT has not. In *The Arm of the Starfish*—a swift, cloak-and-dagger, jet-age novel with an atmosphere somewhat reminiscent of Graham Greene's *The Third Man*—the hero's problem is to tell good and evil apart. Evil can have an attractive face; can cast doubt on good. The hero, Adam, is dazzled by sophisticated and 'spectacularly beautiful' Carolyn Cutter, who turns out to be on the wrong side; and he is warned by her against Canon Tallis, who in fact is good. Here it seems that the bad side aims to make corrupt use of scientific discovery, and the real triumph of good is not so much the defeat of villainy as the decision of the scientist Dr O'Keefe to use the results of his research to benefit bad girl Carolyn. For, as Adam says, 'if you're going to care about the fall of the sparrow you can't pick and choose who's going to be the sparrow'.

In *The Young Unicorns*, Miss L'Engle's Upper West Side story, the author seems to me to extend still farther her sense of evil as a positive thing and, perhaps, in some ways the mirror-image of good. Here much of the action takes place in a great cathedral and it turns out that the apparent Bishop—whose name, significantly, is Fall—had become a figure of evil, in league with delinquent gangs and with a villainous scientist prepared to misuse the laser device. Victory goes to the innocent: to the Austins and their friends, especially a young girl blinded in a sinister accident with the laser. The innocent, it seems, are protected by their innocence; the blind girl's blindness enables her, at the climax of the story, to save herself and others by finding a way through a warren of underground passages.

Miss L'Engle, it will be seen, has the nerve to present moral issues in black and white rather than in a steady, understanding grey. Audacity is something she never lacks. In *A Wrinkle in Time* she does not hesitate to enlist the greatest names on 'our' side in the battle against the powers of darkness:

'Who have our fighters been?' Calvin asked . . .

'Jesus!' Charles Wallace said. 'Why, of course, Jesus!'

'Of course!' Mrs Whatsit said. 'Go on, Charles, love. There were others. All your great artists. They've been lights for us to see by.'

'Leonardo da Vinci?' Calvin suggested tentatively. 'And Michelangelo?'

'And Shakespeare,' Charles Wallace called out, 'and Bach! And Pasteur and Madame Curie and Einstein!'

Now Calvin's voice rang with confidence. 'And Schweitzer and Gandhi and Buddha and Beethoven and Rembrandt and St Francis!'

Most writers would, I think, be embarrassed by the thought of calling so magnificent a roll of honour in their pages, but Miss L'Engle has the wholehearted conviction that enables her to do this and get away with it. There is daring of another kind in the splendid yet shocking scene in *The Young Unicorns* when the robed Bishop is seen, resplendent on his throne and surrounded by young hoodlums, holding court in an abandoned underground railway station.

These three novels have their faults. In all of them the action is at times confusing. In *A Wrinkle in Time*, one sometimes has a sense of the derivative or second-rate, as for instance in the descriptions of the zombie planet. The outsize brain, pulsing away on a dais and controlling everything, could provoke a giggle rather than a shudder. In *The Arm of the Starfish*, the scenes between the hero and the siren Carolyn are quite unconvincing; surely no American student could be so mawkish. In *The Young Unicorns*, the sweetness of the relationships among the Austins and their friends gives a feeling that somewhere inside an apparently tough book is a soft centre. On the other hand, Miss L'Engle knows how to tell a story and can keep the reader turning the pages. She may confuse or embarrass or irritate him, but she is unlikely to bore him.

Though she has other work to her name, the five novels discussed in this essay seem to me to be, so far, Miss L'Engle's main achievement in writing for children. As I have suggested, they have many imperfections. And yet I find her an extraordinarily interesting writer. She aims high, and will risk a few misses for the sake of the hits. She is not afraid of strong feeling. She does not mind being clever, or even showing off a bit, as in a display of quotations in a variety of languages in *A Wrinkle in Time*. She is various, unpredictable, full of ideas. Sometimes one wants to go through her books crossing bits out, but one realizes that they would be diminished rather than improved by such treatment. They are what they are: faulty but intriguing, irritating but likeable, unsatisfactory in various ways but stimulating to the mind and the emotions. They belong, I believe, in the small, frustrating but fascinating category of good bad books.

Here are some extracts from a paper given by Miss L'Engle at the annual conference of the Louisiana Library Association in 1964:

The hardest part of writing a book is making yourself sit down at the typewriter and bat out a first page, any kind of first page, knowing that it will be changed over and over again before the book is done. But there will never be a book without this rough beginning . . .

In using words and in trying to communicate we are trying to speak a universal language—what Erich Fromm calls *The Forgotten Language*, the language of fairy tale, dream, parable, myth, and the language most writers inevitably stumble into, usually in a form more acceptable to children than to adults, because in trying to speak it we must become again like children in their first excited discovery of words.

Not long ago I spoke at a girls' boarding school where I was asked over and over again, 'Why do you write for children?' My immediate, instinctive response was, 'I don't.' Of course I don't. I don't suppose most children's writers do. But the girls weren't going to let me get away with it so easily. I had to try to explain, to myself as well as to the girls.

I write because I am stuck with being a writer. This is what I am. It is the premise on which my whole life is built. There have been occasions when a puritan conscience has impelled me to try to spend more time and creative energy on such things as making better pie crust and moving furniture to get at every speck of dust. I have finally, and with humility, learned that I am a better wife and a better mother when I am writing than when I am baking; and if my children often have to call, 'Mother, get away from the typewriter, the peas are burning,' I still have more time to give them my undivided attention when I am in the midst of an exciting sequence in a book than when I am grappling with the mysteries of the vacuum cleaner.

But why, specifically, are half my books children's books? the girls wanted to know. 'First of all,' I told them, 'you have to write whatever book it is that wants to be written. And then, if it's going to be too difficult for grownups, you write it for children.' This is usually good for a gasp and then maybe a disbelieving laugh, but it is absolutely true.

So I am asked to explain, and I find explanations difficult. Here are two words that may provide a key: childish and childlike. Just as there is all the difference in the world between a person who is child*ish* and a person who is child*like*, so there is all the difference in the world between a book that is child*ish* and a book that is child*like*.

A childish book, like a childish person, is limited, unspontaneous, closed in . . . But the childlike book, like the childlike person, breaks out of all boundaries. And joy is the key. Several years ago we took our children through Monticello, and I remember the feeling we all had of the *fun* Jefferson must have had with his experiments, his preposterous perpetual clock, for instance: what sheer, childlike delight it must have given him. Perhaps Lewis Carroll was really happy only when he was with children, especially when he was writing for them. Joy sparks the pages of *Alice*, and how much more profound it is than most of his ponderous works for grownups.

But did Lewis Carroll, do any children's writers, ever sit down at a desk thinking, 'I am going to write a book for children?'

I doubt it. I think the children's writer writes, primarily, for himself. He clarifies things for himself, not by wrapping them up in tight and tidy patterns, but in opening himself up to them. One of the greatest joys of writing is seeing words we never expected appear on the page. But first the writer must go through the fear that accompanies all beginnings, out onto the open road of adventure where the forgotten language is understood. Then, and then only, is he freed to communicate what he has seen to others.

Madeleine L'Engle

Bibliography

Miss L'Engle's books for children include:

AND BOTH WERE YOUNG. Lothrop, 1949.
CAMILLA DICKINSON. Simon and Schuster, 1951.
MEET THE AUSTINS. Vanguard, 1960; Collins, 1966.
A WRINKLE IN TIME. Farrar, Straus and Giroux, 1962; Longman, 1963.
THE MOON BY NIGHT. Farrar, Straus and Giroux, 1963.
TWENTY-FOUR DAYS BEFORE CHRISTMAS. Farrar, Straus and Giroux, 1964.
THE ARM OF THE STARFISH. Farrar, Straus and Giroux, 1966.
JOURNEY WITH JONAH. Farrar, Straus and Giroux, 1967.
PRELUDE. Vanguard, 1968; Gollancz, 1970.
THE YOUNG UNICORNS. Farrar, Straus and Giroux, 1968; Gollancz, 1969.
DANCE IN THE DESERT. Farrar, Straus and Giroux, 1969; Longman, 1969.
LINES SCRIBBLED ON AN ENVELOPE, AND OTHER POEMS. Farrar, Straus and Giroux, 1969.

William Mayne

William Mayne was born in Yorkshire in 1928, the eldest of five children of a doctor and nurse. He went to Canterbury Cathedral Choir School, which provided the setting for four of his books. Since leaving school he has taught for brief periods, travelled, and worked for a year with the BBC, but mostly he has been a full-time writer. He has lived for some years in the village of Thornton Rust, overlooking Wensleydale, and has built himself a house there.

His first book, Follow the Footprints, *was published in 1953. Among subsequent novels have been* A Swarm in May *(1955),* A Grass Rope, *which won the Carnegie Medal for 1957,* Earthfasts *(1966), and* Ravensgill *(1970). He has also written stories and picture-book texts for young children.*

Next to that of Enid Blyton, the name of William Mayne is probably the one most likely to start an argument about children's books. It is much the same argument, though approached from opposite ends. Enid Blyton's books are popular with great numbers of children, but deeply disliked by adults who care about books. William Mayne appeals strongly to adults with an interest in children's books, but frequently fails to arouse a response in children, even highly intelligent ones. 'A marvellous children's writer for grown-ups,' I have heard it said of him, 'but is he such a marvellous children's writer for children?'

I do not myself see how it can be held against a writer that his work is a minority taste. It may affect his pocket, or his publisher's pocket, or the number of copies of his books that a library needs to order, but it does not diminish the merit of the books themselves. This is one of the points at which our frequent confusion of standards can be seen. And even if I make the deliberate switch from 'what the book is' to 'what the book can do for the child', I can find no method of weighing a superficial pleasure given to many thousands against a deep personal experience which may come only to a few. My own conviction is that if a book opens windows in the imagination of only one child, it has justified its existence.

William Mayne has never made any concessions to the lazy or inattentive reader; he has never written the fully-automated book. In any case, we cannot all like the same things, and even among books of comparable merit there must always be some that strike a more popular note than others. Nevertheless, the impression of Mayne as a writer of somewhat rarefied excellence – one who operates at a high literary altitude where the air is thin – still persists, and may have some justification. Re-reading many of his novels in a short time – after having previously read and admired them individually at the time of publication – I am inclined to feel that Mayne as a writer has a characteristic which deprives his work of a substantial and vital element.

This, I think, is a tendency to shy away from the passions. Children feel strong emotion and can be deeply conscious of strong emotion in others, even when it is not understood. Life without it is less than the whole of life. Mayne is aware of the passions, most notably so in *Ravensgill*, but even there he appears to define deep feeling by drawing round its edges rather than plunging in. One senses in *Ravensgill* that the air is full of old guilt and fear, grievance and feud and loss; but one is never there in the middle, experiencing these things. Pity and terror are rare in Mayne's books; the expression of love, in any of its many forms, is to the best of my recollection absent. To say this is not to make an adverse criticism of any book. *Ravensgill* seems to me exceptionally fine, and I do not suggest that the author could or should have written it differently. But there is a limitation here. I suspect that it is a lack of robustness and of red corpuscle in Mayne's work which often causes it to make a less satisfying impact than that of writers who are more crude in their perceptions and far less gifted artistically.

There is no lack of evidence on which Mayne's progress can be judged. For a 'quality' writer he is remarkably prolific. Between 1953 and 1970 he published some forty books: an average of more than two a year. He started young and shows every sign of reaching his century. His first book, *Follow the Footprints*, published when he was only twenty-five, is in many ways characteristic, and could not be mistaken for the work of anyone else. It is an elaborate treasure-hunt in which a mystery from the past is solved and reputedly supernatural phenomena turn out to have a rational, though highly complicated, explanation. This is not yet vintage Mayne—he has done the same thing in several later books and done it better. But it is full of typical Mayne dialogue: oblique, elliptical, or going off at curious tangents.

> 'I can see the sea,' said Caroline. 'Quite easily.'
>
> Everybody came to look. To the south, at the farthest edge of sight there was the thin blue shading that showed the sea, and beyond that the sky.
>
> 'Funny how you can always see something,' said Andrew. 'Even if it's not really there, like the sky.'
>
> 'The sky's there,' said Caroline.
>
> 'It isn't,' said Andrew. 'You can see it, but there's nothing there.'
>
> 'That's the sea all right,' said Daddy. 'And after that there's Ireland, then America.'
>
> 'Then Australia,' said Andrew. 'Then Siberia, then we get back here again. So we're really looking at the back of our own heads.'

I did not read *Follow the Footprints* when it first came out, so I cannot say how it seemed when Mayne was new and when the number of good current children's books was much smaller. I do, however, recall the first appearance of *A Swarm in May* (1955), which seemed then, and seems now, an outstanding piece of work. In this novel, set in a cathedral choir school based on the one he had attended as a boy, Mayne created or re-created a closed, complete and satisfying world, in which a large cast of characters was clearly distinguished, and in which a story was clearly told and a mystery satisfyingly solved. And behind these individuals, behind the daily life of school and the puzzle from the past, emerging out of the mist to dwarf them all, was the cathedral itself. Indeed, the cathedral seemed in the end to become the frame of the story: a frame filled with cathedral space, a space filled with cathedral music, with the choir's singing and Dr Sunderland's organ-playing. It is hard to fault *A Swarm in May*.

Within its limits – and in this case I believe the limits were a source of strength – it is as near to perfection as any children's book of its decade. Even *Tom's Midnight Garden* is of no greater formal excellence, although it has a depth which *A Swarm in May* lacks. But then, the latter was a young man's book; indeed, it gives the impression that it might have been written by a marvellously talented schoolboy, a literary Mozart.

In the books which followed, Mayne seemed to be elegantly treading water. Individually his books were of obvious distinction and were duly acclaimed, but, collectively, they began to add up to a disappointment. Three more choir-school books – *Choristers' Cake* (1956), *Cathedral Wednesday* (1960) and *Words and Music* (1963) – followed *A Swarm in May* and added very little to the original achievement. There were more treasure-hunts, too. *A Grass Rope* (1957) won the Carnegie Medal which to my mind should have gone to *A Swarm in May*. I do not think it is Mayne at his very best, though there is excellence in its evocation of that Yorkshire dalescape which is Mayne's own and in which several later books have been set. With *The Thumbstick* (1959), *The Rolling Season* (1960) and *The Twelve Dancers* (1962) the treasure-hunting element became ever more convoluted, and the last of these books is more an ingenious puzzle than a story.

In 1964 and 1965 a change of direction came with *Sand* and *Pig in the Middle*. These were about the everyday lives of boys and young adolescents, doing quite ordinary things with no elaborate mysteries to be solved. The setting of *Sand* – a Yorkshire coast town that is being slowly suffocated by sand-dunes – is splendidly drawn; sand can almost be felt on the reader's eyeballs; and there is a memorable relationship between the hero and the elder sister who refers to him with distaste in the third person: '"Look at him laying the jam on," said Alice. "Doesn't it disgust you, Mother?"' Here too – a new departure for Mayne – we have a group of boys who are desperately keen to get to know some girls, though they don't quite know how to set about it. *Sand* comes close to being a very good story, but is marred to my mind by a seemingly-endless account of an attempt by the boys to excavate the tracks of an old narrow-gauge railway. Their persistence in this pointless task is entirely convincing, but the description of it comes to share its own pointlessness; and although the excavation leads to the pleasing climax in which the boys dump a huge, supposedly-prehistoric skeleton in the girls' school yard by way of getting acquainted, it takes a long and weary time to reach this point. I have heard praise of *Pig in the Middle*, a story about boys in an inner-city district who try to rehabilitate an old barge; but it seems to me that Mayne is not at home in this setting, and its greyness has communicated itself to the book.

At this stage, with the new writers of the 1960s becoming prominent, it seemed that Mayne was almost becoming a back number. But in 1966 he published *Earthfasts*: an extraordinarily fine book in which at last he surpassed his early work. I believe that in *Earthfasts* there is an element of response to the novels of Alan Garner. At last Mayne makes use of the supernatural, which previously he seemed to have avoided, and he uses it superbly. In Garner's manner he brings the fantasy-world into the here-and-now; and to make it more credible he has as his main characters two modern, scientifically-minded schoolboys who look for rational explanations of everything. When *they* are convinced that the impossible has happened, we are all convinced.

On a Yorkshire hillside one evening, David and Keith see a stirring in the turf and hear a drumming; there's movement as if someone was getting out of bed, there's light, 'increasing light, pure and mild and bleak,' and out of the hillside marches a drummer-boy, who'd marched into it in 1742 and hadn't been heard of since. He carries a candle that burns with a cold, white, unchanging flame, and he has been searching for the supposed burial-place of King Arthur and his knights. The drummer is a matter-of-fact Yorkshire lad, and he marches off to look for the cottage where he used to live—which is still there—and the girl he left behind him—who is not. When the boys convince him of his situation he doesn't make too much fuss but marches back into the hillside.

The drummer-boy's appearance resulted from something like a geological fault in time. Over the next few weeks there are strange phenomena: huge footprints appear, a wild boar roams the streets, prehistoric stones move from their places—but are they stones or giants? Strangest yet, David, by looking into that cold candlelight, acquires some kind of second sight, more a danger than a gift; and one day he vanishes from the earth—struck, people think, by lightning. From here the story, like some swift, intricate dance, swirls eye-defeatingly faster and faster until the moment when Keith, replacing the cold-flamed candle in the centre of a round table in an underground cavern, stops everything, turns moving figures into stalactite and stalagmite, and seals up the fault in time.

The sheer sweep of *Earthfasts*, swift and wide and totally under control, has never been matched by Mayne. It has its flaws at the level of simple surface probability—surely two boys finding themselves in possession of an ever-burning cold candle would have taken it straight to be analysed—but it marks a breakthrough, and it remains, in 1970, its author's best book. It also seems to have begun a new lease of artistic life. In 1968 Mayne took up another time theme, but played it the other way round, with his present-day characters journeying into the past. This was *Over the Hills and Far Away*, in which Dolly and Andrew and Sara, pony-trekking on a visit to their Gran, find themselves switched into post-Roman Britain, into a tale of old unhappy far-off things that they can't understand or even really believe in. And Sara, who has flaming red hair, is looked on by the tribesmen among whom she finds herself as a witch, a saviour, a sacrifice. *Over the Hills and Far Away* is notable for an outstandingly clear, almost transparent, style of writing, and for the effective contrast between the fluid, dreamlike nature of the action and the enduring solidity of the Yorkshire landscape through which it moves. *Ravensgill* (1970) is set, yet again, in the Yorkshire dales, and at first sight has a resemblance to Mayne's work of the *Grass Rope* period, a dozen years earlier. Here are families on two farms, estranged by an unsolved crime of half a century ago. Here is an elaborate and ingenious solution to the mystery. But there is a sombre note in *Ravensgill* which is new to Mayne; and the dominant character, Grandma, the impetuous girl who lost her man long years ago and has grown into a foolish, pathetic, but spirited old woman is one that I would once have thought outside his range.

William Mayne is a writer with striking strengths and weaknesses. He has a genuinely distinguished, if sometimes unduly whimsical, mind. He writes superbly. He can evoke a landscape, a time of day or year, a kind of weather, the feeling of the way things are, as in *Sand*:

> The shirt was made of cold cloth and frozen buttons. It lay on Ainsley's bed like a drift of snow. The cold spring wind blew the curtains and moaned under the door. Ainsley stroked the shirt. It had been starched with ice.

He has an unfailing gift for the precise and vivid simile:

> Her heart banged in her like a wildcat in a sack.

> The flame perched on the wick like a bright bird.

These examples are both from *Over the Hills and Far Away*. Occasionally he can lapse into archness, however, as in *Ravensgill*:

> It was Sunday sunshine, that seems to be as hot as any other, but is not doing any work with its heat, because of the day.

He has a fine imagination, and a gift for story construction and narration when he cares to use it, which is not always. If he feels so disposed he will turn aside from his story to chase images like butterflies, snatching significant and insignificant detail alike from the air. He will allow the action of a story to mount towards climax and then, casually and disappointingly, let it down. His plot structure may sag in the middle, as in *Sand*; and he seems unworried by disconcerting shifts of viewpoint, as in *Over the Hills*, which has a complete change of cast after the first fifty pages.

He is a notable writer of dialogue, and, like many who excel in this field, appears to have a gift of mimicry. In *The Twelve Dancers* almost all the characters are Welsh, and although not a word of Welsh is spoken, their English is Welsh English. His ear is unfailing and one hardly needs to be told that he is a musical man. He knows how things are done, and can tell you; he seems to have an instinctive understanding of all trades, their gear and tackle and trim. But his books are not notable for their characters. Between Dr Sunderland, the rumbling-voiced choirmaster of *A Swarm in May*, and Grandma in *Ravensgill* fifteen years later, I find that few Mayne characters spring unbidden to mind. On looking through the books, one finds many who are well drawn, and hardly one who fails to ring true, but few who come vigorously off the page with a life of their own.

Mayne has written that 'the best part of a book is the plot . . . I don't bother with the characters until I have begun'. To my mind this is a weakness. There are only a few basic plots, and they have all been used again and again. Character is infinite, and, for my money, characters make novels. But, on the whole, Mayne children mostly resemble other Mayne children. Of the numerous mothers and fathers, the only one who stays firmly in my memory is Marlene's sharp, narrow, down-to-earth mother in *The Twelve Dancers*, who sends three-year-old small brother Porky to school to get him out of the way, but grouses at having to pay dinner-money: 'He can't eat a shilling a day if he tried.'

The reluctance, noted earlier, to become involved with any depth of feeling may have something to do with Mayne's relative failure in the area of characterization. Often one feels that the emotional life of his characters is weak or is simply left blank, and they are correspondingly enfeebled.

Interestingly, William Mayne's books for younger children about everyday life are among the best in that rather barren genre. A pleasure in fantasy can be shared by writer, parent and quite small child; but most authors seem to find that the restricted range of a child's experience makes it difficult to tell a worthwhile story for the younger age-groups about actual life. *No More School* (1965), which tells how Ruth and Shirley keep the village school unofficially open while the teacher Miss Oldroyd is ill, is a small gem of a story, for all that there is nothing in it beyond the understanding of a child of eight or nine. *The Fishing Party* (1960), in which a class of children is taken to catch crayfish and cook them on the spot, is simple, unaffected, and totally absorbing, whatever the reader's age. *The Toffee Join* (1968) is a story about three sets of cousins and the contributions they take to the sweetmaking of their joint Granny. It is perfectly on the level of a very small child, and it is perfectly and properly serious.

Mayne's special quality as a writer for young children is that he never sees things with the used adult eye, or fails to see them because of the preoccupied adult mind. Everything is experienced afresh. He notes exactly the things that children do but adults have forgotten:

> 'It's raining,' said Diana. She huffed her breath on to the window and drew on the steamy mark with her finger. She drew a smile and a nose and two eyes, but before she could draw the chin and the hair and the ears the mark had gone away.

That is the opening of *The Toffee Join*. A few pages on, Mother is giving the children treacle in a polythene bag. It sits 'all smiling in the clear plastic', and each child in turn has to have the cold clingy bag pressed against the back of its neck. There is never any condescension, and nothing is dull or commonplace about the small details of daily life as seen by William Mayne.

His principal work, nevertheless, consists of his numerous novels for older children. They are for the most part individual, original, enjoyable, admirable. Their flavour is unlike that of anything else. Some of the recent books have shown the author reaching out towards new achievement: *Earthfasts*, *Over the Hills and Far Away* and *Ravensgill*, especially, show signs of a maturity as a writer which had been long delayed after early brilliance. In spite of having written forty books, Mayne still has plenty of time on his side, and there is every reason to suppose he will go on filling out as a writer. In 1955 one felt of the author of *A Swarm in May* that he might do anything. In 1970 one feels much the same about the author of *Ravensgill*.

William Mayne writes:

My ways of doing things are either so boring that they don't bear retailing, or so private that even I do not know about them. I don't see why anyone shouldn't do it, because it's reasonably easy, but if I say so then anyone thinks I am being arrogant. The boring bits are the getting up every twenty-four hours or so and walking to the typewriter, or pen, or dictating machine, or telephone if the controls of other devices are too complex that day, and uttering a few words. All I can consciously do is be present, somewhat but not toowhat awake, clothed and (by various tests taken daily) sane enough to mix with humanity. It is possible to be too insane, relatively speaking; that is, sane by some median internal judgement, not having become proud, or certain, or angry, not hating or envying or assessing. I am only a lens for others, and I must do my best not to distort or colour. My responsibility for being the *lens sana* goes only so far, though, as far as seeing that what I say is what I see. I am not responsible for what I see, though I can be blamed for what I look at. And since I am not responsible there I am not responsible either for what anyone else sees. If the lens is astigmatic I may not know it; chromatic aberrations too are not detectable from within the organism, where I am *in corpore sano*, perhaps, perhaps not.

I have no ambitions in writing. I may have a few plots in mind at any moment, but that's not ambition. My daily care is not for *what* I may do, but *how* I may do it. My future writing is not of interest to me, because interest in it now might be a substitute for experiencing it then, when the time comes to write it. I am quite out of the habit of telling anyone what I am doing, have done, or hope to do. A thing once said ought not to be said again, if possible, and to say now would preclude later writing; to think now might do the same. An attitude of mind like that is probably a hindrance to writing, and a positive impediment to plotting. I must use some other method. I am not clear what it is, however. I can only abstract the observed cycle, that I think of something, then I write it down, then I don't think of anything for some time, and then I think of something else, and so on. Actually of course I am thinking of several things at once, but usually only writing down one at a time. I don't like writing. I decided on it as a career when I was too young to realize I would not grow out of the dislike, but I have never had enough imagination to think of another living. But I suppose the same rules would apply whatever I did: the rules we all are aware of.

William Mayne

Bibliography

FOLLOW THE FOOTPRINTS. Oxford University Press, 1953.
THE WORLD UPSIDE DOWN. Oxford University Press, 1954.
A SWARM IN MAY. Oxford University Press, 1955.
CHORISTERS' CAKE. Oxford University Press, 1956.
THE MEMBER FOR THE MARSH. Oxford University Press, 1956.
THE BLUE BOAT. Oxford University Press, 1957; Dutton, 1960.
A GRASS ROPE. Oxford University Press, 1957; Dutton, 1962.
UNDERGROUND ALLEY. Oxford University Press, 1958; Dutton, 1961.
THE THUMBSTICK. Oxford University Press, 1959.
CATHEDRAL WEDNESDAY. Oxford University Press, 1960.
THE FISHING PARTY. Hamish Hamilton, 1960.
THE ROLLING SEASON. Oxford University Press, 1960.
THE CHANGELING. Oxford University Press, 1961; Dutton, 1963.
THE GLASS BALL. Hamish Hamilton, 1961; Dutton, 1962.
SUMMER VISITORS. Oxford University Press, 1961.
THE LAST BUS. Hamish Hamilton, 1962.
THE TWELVE DANCERS. Hamish Hamilton, 1962.
THE MAN FROM THE NORTH POLE. Hamish Hamilton, 1963.
ON THE STEPPING STONES. Hamish Hamilton, 1963.
PLOT NIGHT. Hamish Hamilton, 1963; Dutton, 1968.
WORDS AND MUSIC. Hamish Hamilton, 1963.
A DAY WITHOUT WIND. Hamish Hamilton, 1964; Dutton, 1964.
A PARCEL OF TREES. Hamish Hamilton, 1964.
SAND. Hamish Hamilton, 1964; Dutton, 1965.
WATER BOATMAN. Hamish Hamilton, 1964.
WHISTLING RUFUS. Hamish Hamilton, 1964; Dutton, 1965.
THE BIG WHEEL AND THE LITTLE WHEEL. Hamish Hamilton, 1965.
NO MORE SCHOOL. Hamish Hamilton, 1965.
PIG IN THE MIDDLE. Hamish Hamilton, 1965; Dutton, 1966.
EARTHFASTS. Hamish Hamilton, 1966; Dutton, 1967.
THE OLD ZION. Hamish Hamilton, 1966; Dutton, 1967.

ROOFTOPS. Hamish Hamilton, 1966.

THE BATTLEFIELD. Hamish Hamilton, 1967; Dutton, 1967.

THE BIG EGG. Hamish Hamilton, 1967.

THE HOUSE ON FAIRMOUNT. Hamish Hamilton, 1968; Dutton, 1968.

OVER THE HILLS AND FAR AWAY. Hamish Hamilton, 1968; Dutton, 1968, as THE HILL ROAD.

THE TOFFEE JOIN. Hamish Hamilton, 1968.

THE YELLOW AEROPLANE. Hamish Hamilton, 1968.

THE GOBBLING BILLY (with Dick Caesar). Brockhampton Press, 1969. (Originally published by Gollancz in 1959 under the names Dynely James and R. D. Caesar.)

RAVENSGILL. Hamish Hamilton, 1970; Dutton, 1970.

ROYAL HARRY. Hamish Hamilton, 1971; Dutton, 1971.

A GAME OF DARK. Hamish Hamilton, 1971; Dutton, 1971.

Willaim Mayne has edited the following anthologies:

THE HAMISH HAMILTON BOOK OF KINGS (with Eleanor Farjeon). Hamish Hamilton, 1964; Walck, 1965, as A CAVALCADE OF KINGS.

THE HAMISH HAMILTON BOOK OF QUEENS (with Eleanor Farjeon). Hamish Hamilton, 1965; Walck, 1965, as A CAVALCADE OF QUEENS.

THE HAMISH HAMILTON BOOK OF HEROES. Hamish Hamilton, 1967; Dutton, 1968, as WILLIAM MAYNE'S BOOK OF HEROES.

THE HAMISH HAMILTON BOOK OF GIANTS. Hamish Hamilton, 1968; Dutton, 1969, as WILLIAM MAYNE'S BOOK OF GIANTS.

GHOSTS. Hamish Hamilton, 1971; Nelson, New York, 1971.

William Mayne's short stories for children include *The Long Night* in FIVE MORE (Blackwell, 1957), *Thirteen O'Clock* in ANOTHER SIX (Blackwell, 1959) and *A Haunted Terrace* in THE FABER BOOK OF STORIES, edited by Kathleen Lines (Faber and Faber, 1960).

Andre Norton

Andre Norton was born in Cleveland, Ohio, and worked for a number of years in the Cleveland Public Library as a children's librarian. During World War II she worked as a special librarian for a citizenship project in Washington, D.C., and at the Library of Congress. In addition she was at one time manager of a bookstore.

During and after the war Miss Norton wrote a number of historical and adventure stories. Since 1951 she has produced mainly science fiction. She became a full-time writer in 1952, the year in which her first science fiction novel, Star Man's Son, *was published. Many science fiction adventures have followed, as well as historical novels and fantasies.*

Andre Norton is a prolific writer who has produced more than sixty books, latterly at the rate of three or four a year. Her work includes stories, science fiction, historical novels and fantasy, but she is best known – and in England almost entirely known – as a science fiction writer. That is the side of her work which will be dealt with here. None of Miss Norton's historical novels is in print in England at the time of writing. Three fantasies – *Steel Magic* (1965), *Octagon Magic* (1967) and *Fur Magic* (1968) – have been published both in the United States and Britain. Although the fantasies and historical stories have merit, it seems to me that the science fiction is the most interesting part of her work and the basis of her reputation.

Miss Norton's science fiction books are, in the main, 'space opera': stories of galactic and inter-galactic adventure. This is the category of science fiction which is least likely to be found acceptable by the literati. Space opera is associated with pulp magazines, and is apt to be written off on superficial inspection as wild, undisciplined stuff, all about clashing fleets of spaceships, battles with bug-eyed monsters, death and destruction by ray-gun: action of meaningless violence in settings which are spatially enormous but imaginatively minute. Andre Norton has used the standard ingredients of space opera without undue inhibition, but they are not the be-all and end-all of her work. The sheer size of her world, which is infinitely extended in time and space, and in which nothing is outside the bounds of possibility, is matched by the size of the themes she tackles. She has had her artistic failures – quite a number of them – but she has had her successes, too.

She is a highly professional writer, and has always paid full attention to the need to hold the reader, including the young reader who is simply in it for the story. Incident follows incident, sometimes coming so thick and fast as to obscure the main line of the plot. But there is always something beyond the immediate action to be reached for and thought about. Miss Norton's sources of inspiration include Greek and Roman history as well as archaeology and anthropology, myth and folklore. She is not much interested in science-for-science's-sake, and obviously has a strong awareness of the menace of uncontrolled or miscontrolled technological development. One subject which deeply interests her and which occurs again and again is telepathy, often as a means of communication between man and animal. She is also fascinated by mutations and new forms of life, although she does not seem to me to have overcome the problem imposed by the limits of human imagination: we cannot conceive of *really* new forms of life, we tend to think of variations on forms we know, and the result is often ludicrous.

Miss Norton's books have not been published in England in the order in which they were written. Her first science fiction stories – though they were by no means her first novels – were the four 'Star' books: *Star Man's Son*, *Star Rangers*, *Star Guard*, and *Star Gate*. The title of *Star Man's Son* (1952) sounds like that of a sequel, but it is not. It is a fairly straightforward story, set in a post-cataclysmic world – our own – where a few small communities survive in a primitive way, and in which the hero sets out to look for a lost city which is rumoured to be safe from radiation. The Norton interest in telepathy and mutation is already present; the hero is himself a mutant and has a telepathic relationship with a giant cat; but the book does not have the range and imaginative power of later ones.

The other three 'Star' books, while all set in the future, have classical associations. A foreword to *Star Rangers* (1953) refers to the legend of the Roman Emperor who simultaneously demonstrated his absolute power and the loyalty of his legions by sending one of them to march to the end of the world. The legion duly set out eastward into Asia and was never heard of again. Miss Norton's book looks many thousands of years ahead to the declining years of a kind of galactic Roman Empire, in which a stellar patrol of men loyal to service tradition and discipline is sent on a fool's errand in an ill-maintained ship to a forgotten corner of the galaxy. This is a big advance on Miss Norton's first science fiction novel; it is probably the best of the early group and certainly the one I would recommend for sampling. Apart from the Roman analogy, her interest in telepathy is developed: there are now 'sensitives' at different levels on the scale of extra-sensory perception, and, at one point, a literal battle of wills is described with some success. An unexpected twist at the end comes when the forgotten planet turns out to be Terra, or Earth, from which space colonization began many thousands of years ago, and on which a new start now appears to be possible. A curious minor detail is the use of broken-down surnames of today for several characters: Jaksan, Smitt, Kartr.

The third book, *Star Guard* (1955), is also based on a Roman Empire situation – in this case a decadent central power-structure trying to hold down vigorous barbarians from Earth – but its main action, the retreat of a legion, has a Greek source, for it is in effect a retelling of the *Anabasis* of Xenophon. The fourth, *Star Gate* (1958), begins with the withdrawal of the wise and great Star Lords from a planet which they have raised from savagery to a feudal civilization. Although this hints at the departure of the legions, the feeling of the story is medieval. And the philosophic interest is something different again. It lies in an exploration of time theory: could there be a parallel world, also existing 'now', in which things have developed differently? The assumption is made that there could; and the 'star gate' is a device for transposing into and out of it. (Incidentally, if time as a single straight line is the fourth dimension, then a time in which parallel developments could take place would require a fifth dimension, that of space-in-time. Miss Norton's field of speculation is wide indeed.) But although Andre Norton is prepared to mix the remote past with the distant future and the might-have-been, her action has to be on a comprehensible human scale, and tends to take place on a reasonably familiar-seeming earth-type planet on which people can move and breathe as we do. The hero of *The Beast Master* (1959) and its sequel *Lord of Thunder* (1962) is, by ancestry, a Navajo Indian, and although he lives at a time when this earth has been reduced to a blue radioactive cinder, the territory he inhabits on another planet is remarkably like the American West.

Of the later Norton science fiction books, which cannot all be discussed in this small amount of space, the most imaginative, though not the most successful, is *Judgment on Janus* (1963), in which the hero finds himself drawn through inward change into membership of an infinitely-remote, green-skinned tree people. There is a sequel, *Victory on Janus* (1966), from which come these reflections as the hero lies on the rich soil of a woodland glade:

> Iftsiga, Iftcan—the home Forest—his mind kept returning to the green there. Spring, and the rise of renewing sap—the awakening of Iftin bodies. Summer, with the long, beautiful nights for hunting, for living. Fall, with the last securing of the Crowns, the coming of the need for sleep. Winter, when one's body was cradled safe within one of the Great Crowns, one's mind travelling—travelling through dreams.

Obviously ventures like this are perilous; a momentary lapse can cause not only loss of credibility but an irretrievable tumble into the comic. And, in fact, the blending in these two books of space technology with the myth-infused forest world of the Iftin does not come off. Too often it produces a result which, instead of the intended dramatic clash, is simply a ludicrous inappropriateness.

The value of old ways of life, of the simple and natural against the sophisticated, artificial and ever-changing, is a frequent issue in Miss Norton's work. It may seem odd to compare her with

Rosemary Sutcliff, but there are curious correspondences. Miss Norton, as the Roman references may already have suggested, is concerned with civilization under the threat of barbarism; but there is also a part of her which sees that civilization is not all, which is deeply aware of instinctual life, is conscious of the rooting of myth in the cycle of life and death, the turning of the seasons. This is true of Miss Sutcliff, too. It is not a contradiction but a proper ambiguity which perhaps is unavoidable in people who both think and feel. And for all their vast spans of time and distance, the Norton novels can often appear to be bounded in a nutshell as well as free of infinite space, for—as in the Janus books—the conflict of tree people with advanced technology may be seen as the externalization of an inner struggle.

Dark Piper (1968) seems to me to be Miss Norton's best book so far, and it draws together most of her enduring themes. In some ways it shows her at her most Roman. The setting is Beltane, an earthlike but little-populated planet housing a small colony of scientists. It has been a backwater during a ten-year inter-galactic war. Now order has broken down and there are piratical bands roaming the skies, ready to take over such outposts and exterminate the inhabitants, as indeed they do on Beltane. But a group of children and young people have been taken to an underground refuge by the far-seeing veteran Griss Lugard. Although he dies, they survive entombment, perils with mutant animals, and plague, and they can continue as the tiny handful of people left alive on an abandoned planet. It is a sombre story, involving the illness and death of a child as well as Lugard's death, and the narrator's conclusion is not too hopeful:

> We realize that those of our small colony coming after us will slip farther and farther down the ladder of civilization, perhaps, in time, to meet others climbing up.

The latter phrase is a reference to the planet's mutant creatures, unaffected by the plague which has killed all humans except the group of children. The piper of the title is Lugard, whose playing enchants birds, beasts and people. Clearly he is a latter-day Pied Piper, though the resemblance is not pushed.

Miss Norton's science fiction books are mainly written in a hard, dry, somewhat impersonal style. Her heroes are young, determined, often afraid but overcoming their fears. They are not characterized in depth, and appear to be blanks for the reader to fill. In the earlier books there are no girls; in the Janus stories there is the forest maiden Illylle, but there is little about her that is flesh and blood. Commonly the heroes are unrooted 'loners' without family or friends, though they make comrades in the course of the action. *Dark Piper* is an exception to nearly all these generalizations. It is a first-person narration, which gives greater immediacy than usual. The children are seen both as distinct individuals and in relationship to the group; and there are real, three-dimensional girl characters in the strong-minded, protective Annet and imaginative Gytha.

Miss Norton handles her gadgetry with great aplomb. She never draws special attention to it; it is simply there. Spaceships are as ordinary as buses. Flitters for moving around in; stunners and blasters and flamers for dealing with your enemies; and 'coms' of all kinds for getting in touch with people are, with countless other devices, casually mentioned in passing without any nudge to the reader. Just occasionally the effects of word-coinage are odd—'he spooned up some lorg sauce and spread it neatly over a horva fritter'—but on the whole this is one of Miss Norton's minor strengths. Few writers are better than she is at inventing things and giving names to them. A more important power, which should not be underrated, is that of telling strong, fast-moving stories.

The Norton universe on the whole is an alarming and hostile one. It is assumed that for thousands of years hence there will be wars and rumours of wars. Peace is there only to be disturbed. Prosperity appears in an unpleasing form on the 'pleasure planet' Korwar, which also houses an intergalactic slum called the Dipple. Corruption and injustice are always around. Nature is red in tooth and claw; man in flamer and blaster. In terms of organized society there seems little to look forward to. It could be of course that strife and confusion are externalized from inner states; divided men who war within themselves will form divided, warring communities; and it is not realistic to expect sudden improvements in human nature.

Miss Norton offers no false comfort in a harsh world. In most of her novels it is quite a triumph even to stay alive. Yet the atmosphere is by no means one of despair. There is always the hope of private happiness, private fulfilment (to be found, as in *Catseye*, in the wild rather than the city), and the development of new faculties, new forms of sympathy and awareness.

Andre Norton writes:

I began writing seriously when I was about sixteen and was on the staff of our high school newspaper. We had a small creative writing class meeting in our own time under an inspired teacher. I was then writing mystery serials, World War I adventure stories and the like. While still in high school I began my first book—a teenage mystery. Eventually after much revision it became my second book to be published. I went to college for a time; then the Depression hit and I left to work in the public library, writing on the side. My mother encouraged me greatly, proof-reading and criticizing my MSS. My first book, a romance set in a mythical kingdom, was published before I was twenty-one.

At the outbreak of World War II, I was asked to write a book for young people on the Underground in Holland; this later earned a plaque from the Netherlands Government. It also led eventually to my best publishing contact. Up to 1950 I wrote historical, mystery and adventure stories. Since 1951 I have been writing mainly science fiction. I like writing fantasy and science fiction because the imagination is allowed full play and there are few limits placed on the type or amount of action allowed.

I do a great deal of research for each book, having an extensive personal library to draw upon. Folklore, natural history, history, archaeology, anthropology, native religions etc all go into my background reading. I try to get material into a book which will make the reader want to know more about some subject introduced and perhaps do some extra reading of his own thereafter. Writing down is the one thing I abhor. If the story is exciting enough the reader will 'reach' to read it. My public ranges in age from ten to eighty-five, to judge by comments in fan mail.

Uncertain health keeps me very much at my home in Florida.

Andre Norton

I have always loved reading and for a while delighted in needlework, although that is now ruled out because of my eyesight. I am owned and operated – to their advantage – by five cats, who certainly do not allow me to vegetate.

Andre Norton

Bibliography

THE PRINCE COMMANDS. Appleton-Century, 1934.
RALESTONE LUCK. Appleton-Century, 1938.
FOLLOW THE DRUM. William Penn, 1942.
SWORD IS DRAWN. Houghton Mifflin, 1944.
ROGUE REYNARD. Houghton Mifflin, 1947.
SCARFACE. Harcourt Brace, 1948; Methuen, 1950.
SWORD IN SHEATH. Harcourt Brace, 1949; Staples, 1953, as LAND OF THE LOST.
HUON OF THE HORN. Harcourt Brace, 1951.
STAR MAN'S SON. Harcourt Brace, 1952; Gollancz, 1968.
STAR RANGERS. Harcourt Brace, 1953; Gollancz, 1968.
AT SWORD'S POINTS. Harcourt Brace, 1954.
THE STARS ARE OURS! World, 1954.
SARGASSO OF SPACE. Gnome Press, 1955 (under the name Andrew North); Gollancz, 1970.
STAR GUARD. Harcourt Brace, 1955; Gollancz, 1969.
YANKEE PRIVATEER. World, 1955.
CROSSWORDS OF TIME. Ace, 1956.
PLAGUE SHIP. Gnome Press, 1956 (under the name Andrew North).
STAND TO HORSE. Harcourt Brace, 1956.
STAR BORN. World, 1957.
STAR GATE. Harcourt Brace, 1957; Gollancz, 1970.
TIME TRADERS. World, 1958.
THE BEAST MASTER. Harcourt Brace, 1959; Gollancz, 1966.
GALACTIC DERELICT. World, 1959.
SECRET OF THE LOST RACE. Ace, 1959.
VOODOO PLANT. Ace, 1959.
SHADOW HAWK. Harcourt Brace, 1960.
SIOUX. Ace, 1960.
STORM OVER WARLOCK. World, 1960.
CATSEYE. Harcourt Brace, 1961; Gollancz, 1962.
RIDE PROUD REBEL. World, 1961.

Andre Norton

STAR HUNTER. Ace, 1961.
THE DEFIANT AGENTS. World, 1962.
EYE OF THE MONSTER. Ace, 1962.
LORD OF THUNDER. Harcourt Brace, 1962; Gollancz, 1966.
REBEL SPURS. World, 1962.
JUDGMENT ON JANUS. Harcourt Brace, 1963; Gollancz, 1964.
KEY OUT OF TIME. World, 1963.
WITCH WORLD. Ace, 1963.
NIGHT OF MASKS. Harcourt Brace, 1964; Gollancz, 1965.
ORDEAL IN OTHERWHERE. World, 1964.
WEB OF WITCH WORLD. Ace, 1964.
QUEST CROSSTIME. Viking Press, 1965.
STEEL MAGIC. World, 1965; Hamish Hamilton, 1967.
THE X FACTOR. Harcourt Brace, 1965; Gollancz, 1967.
YEAR OF THE UNICORN. Ace, 1965.
MOON OF THREE RINGS. Viking Press, 1966; Longman, 1969.
VICTORY ON JANUS. Harcourt Brace, 1966; Gollancz, 1967.
OCTAGON MAGIC. World, 1967; Hamish Hamilton, 1968.
OPERATION TIME SEARCH. Harcourt Brace, 1967.
WARLOCK OF WITCH WORLD. Ace, 1967.
DARK PIPER. Harcourt Brace, 1968; Gollancz, 1969.
SORCERESS OF WITCH WORLD. Ace, 1968.
ZERO STONE. Viking Press, 1968.
FUR MAGIC. World, 1968; Hamish Hamilton, 1969.
POSTMARKED THE STARS. Harcourt Brace, 1969.
UNCHARTED STARS. Viking Press, 1969.
BERTIE AND MAY (with Bertha Stamm Norton). World, 1970; Hamish Hamilton, 1971.
DREAD COMPANION. Harcourt Brace, 1970.
HIGH SORCERY. Ace, 1970.
ICE CROWN. Viking Press, 1970; Longman, 1971.

Collections edited by Andre Norton include BULLARD OF THE SPACE PATROL (World, 1951), SPACE SERVICE (World, 1953), SPACE PIONEERS (World, 1954) and SPACE POLICE (World, 1956).

Scott O'Dell

Scott O'Dell was born in Los Angeles and went to Stanford University, California. Since then he has studied at the University of Wisconsin, worked in motion pictures in Rome, been a newspaperman and magazine editor, and written several books. His novels for children and young people include Island of the Blue Dolphins, *which won the 1960 Newbery Medal,* The King's Fifth *(1966), and* The Black Pearl *(1967). He lives on the edge of the Pacific at Del Mar, California.*

To readers in Britain, Scott O'Dell seems to live and write on the far western rim of the world: California, Mexico, the Pacific coast and the islands beyond it. And of his first six books for children, five are set in the past and four at least have the flavour of a West that is Indian or Spanish rather than 'American' in the present sense of the word. Their times and places are mysterious and exotic to the insular Englishman – the vague edges of an antique map where dolphins play.

The title of *Island of the Blue Dolphins*, lovely in sound and evocative in all its key words (for the 'blue' transfers itself to the ocean), sums up the attraction of the O'Dell world. But it is not a matter of settings alone; this is an admirable novel; and its successor, *The King's Fifth*, is to my mind even finer, although in Britain it is not well known. The subsequent O'Dell books, up to the time of writing, have been slighter.

Island of the Blue Dolphins (1960) accepts some severe limitations. It is the story of an Indian girl who survives for many years alone on a small and desolate island. For much of its course it has only one human character; so all that large part of the more usual story which depends on dialogue and the interaction of personality is ruled out. The heroine is uneducated, has never been beyond her own tiny territory, has no wider frame of reference; so abstract thought is almost ruled out, too, and figures of speech can only be of the simplest. There is little plot in the conventional sense; the story goes on and on with a good deal of sameness over a long period; its development is in the character of the heroine herself, and this is a theme which it is extremely difficult to make interesting for young readers.

Yet all these limitations have been converted into strengths. The fact that there is only one central character, in this remote and isolated setting, makes identification total; the reader must *be* Karana or the book is meaningless. The telling of the story has a memorable purity to which its fresh direct concreteness contributes as much as the author's excellent ear. And the long, continuous time dimension allows the story to take itself outside our clock-and-calendar system altogether, to complete the islanding of a human being's experience.

A Robinson Crusoe story has of course an appeal of its own which hardly needs to be spelled out. Survival is not an immediate problem at present for most of us in the civilized Western world, but as a theme it still touches upon our deepest inborn instincts and unconscious fears. And the details of survival, so compelling and convincing in *Robinson Crusoe* itself and in all successful Robinsonnades, are absorbing here, and clearly authentic. Last, *Island of the Blue Dolphins* shows a human being in changing relationship to animal life, about which the author obviously knows a great deal. Birds, beasts and fishes are to Karana at first, and to a great extent must continue to be, either things to be hunted or competitors for the means of subsistence; but as she grows she achieves an acceptance of them as fellow-creatures. If there is a key incident in the whole book, it is the one in which she befriends her arch-enemy, the leader of the wild dogs.

It is a story with intrinsic sadness; and not only because of the early death of small brother Ramo and the later death of Karana's only close friend, the dog Rontu. It is immensely sad to lose human company throughout the years of youth. The depth of this loss is hinted at, no more, in the brief, tentative relationship with the girl who accompanies Aleutian hunters to the island; in the tiny touch of vanity over the cormorant-feather skirt; in the girl's marking her face, on being rescued after all those years, with the sign that she is still unmarried. Karana herself is no mere cipher. She has the qualities which are implied and indeed required by her situation; she is strong, sensible, intelligent, resourceful. And while she is unsentimental she can – even in the desolating absence of other human beings – love. A sad story, yes; but the sadness of *Island of the Blue Dolphins* is of a singularly inspiring kind. Among all the Newbery Medal winners there are few better books.

The King's Fifth is a more complex novel, notable among other things for its formal structure. The hero Esteban de Sandoval is in a prison cell in Spanish Mexico, awaiting trial on a charge of having deprived the King of his lawful fifth share in a treasure found far to the north in the unknown lands of New Spain. Interspersing the story of his prison life and trial is Esteban's account, written night by night in his cell, of the events that led up to it; the stories of 'now' and 'then' move forward side by side until they merge in the last chapter, when all has been told and the verdict is handed down.

The underlying story is that of a treasure hunt, in which Esteban, a cartographer, forms one of a small band led by the daring and unscrupulous adventurer Captain Mendoza. The party includes, besides Mendoza's henchmen, a young Indian girl, who is guide and interpreter, and Father Francisco, whose concern is to save souls. As an adventure story – the story of a quest followed by a trek for survival – it does very well; but it is a moral as well as a physical exploration, and there are moral as well as physical events in it.

Treasure is sinister; that is the heart of the matter. It is not merely that treasure is often both hidden and discovered in circumstances of violence and treachery. The truth is also that the hope of great unearned gain can be one of the most corrupting ever to get men in its grip. In *The King's Fifth* there are not so much good and bad characters as the innocent and the corrupted. The guide Zia, who longs to ride a horse and to help with the mapmaker's art, is innocent; so is Father Francisco; so are those Indians to whom gold is mere dirt for which they have no use. The narrator Esteban is less simple. He is led into the quest by his yearning to map what no man has mapped before, and at first devotion to his craft protects him; but the gold which is won at last from an Indian city begins to exert its baneful influence. Mendoza dies, killed by a dog he has trained in savagery;

Zia goes her way, for she sees Esteban becoming another Mendoza; and Esteban finishes in the Inferno, a hot white sandy basin where his last companion, Father Francisco, dies. And only now does he grasp the enormity of the evil burden and tip the gold, enough to make many men rich, into a deep bubbling crater of foul yellow water where it will be lost for ever.

In the parallel story of the consequences – Esteban's imprisonment and trial – the seedy majesty of Spanish law and administration is seen to be similarly corrupted. No one cares for more than the outward forms of justice, but everyone hopes to recover the treasure. Esteban refuses an offer to let him escape, and is ready to serve a three-year sentence in daunting conditions, because freedom for him can now only come through expiation.

The King's Fifth is a sombre and searching book. The two that followed it were less substantial. *The Black Pearl* (1967) is the terse, masculine story of young Ramon, who seized the Pearl of Heaven from the underwater cavern of the great Devilfish; and of Ramon's father, who donated the pearl to the statue of the Madonna in the church on the coast of Lower California, mistakenly thinking to buy divine protection against wind and water; and of the tall-talking Sevillano, who sought to steal the pearl, and fought the Devilfish when it came seeking its own, and died. At last the great pearl, purified now, is placed in the hand of the Madonna-of-the-Sea as a gift of love.

This brief, spare piece of writing (it is of less than novel length, even the fairly short novel length which is now usual in children's books) is something between a fable and a mystery. The greed and presumption of men are punished. Who is Ramon's father to think he can buy the favours of the Almighty, who is the Sevillano to think he can defeat and steal from the mighty Devilfish? Obviously there are symbolisms involved; for while the Madonna is to be adored the dark powers represented by the Devilfish must also be reckoned with. But what are the dark powers, and are they inside or outside the minds of men? That is part of the mystery, and a mystery does not need to have a simple solution, or indeed any solution.

The way the Devilfish dominates this story makes one think of *Moby Dick*; and it is interesting but not surprising that an obsession with that book is the core of O'Dell's next novel. The narrator of *The Dark Canoe* (1968) is Nathan Clegg, cabin boy on board the Nantucket whaler *Alert*; but the dominant character is his elder brother Caleb, part-owner of the ship, who lost his captain's licence in strange circumstances. Caleb resembles Captain Ahab in *Moby Dick*, even to the extent of being similarly scarred and lamed. He resembles Ahab in disposition, too; and there is a description of him 'with his massive head thrown back, black hair, raven black once but now streaked with grey, falling around his face, hands clenched at his sides'. Caleb is not acting the part of Ahab, even though he knows the book by heart; rather, he is 'a man tortured in body and mind who had read Ahab and in time knowingly had become Ahab'.

The wreck of a lost ship is recovered, and a small fortune in ambergris, and the ship's log which clears Caleb of the charge that cost him his licence. On top of all this, Nathan finds a floating chest: the Dark Canoe, such as Queequeg ordered when he thought he was dying, to take him to the archipelagos of heaven, and which Ahab caused to be made into a lifebuoy. And although the ship is ready to sail and the crew restless, Caleb has the dark canoe restored as a buoy, just as in *Moby Dick*. And, resuming the captaincy, he wants to go in search of the White Whale: 'Deep behind his gaze I saw the lurking image of Moby Dick. It was there, it had been there for all the years I remembered, this unloved man's hatred of a world that in its indifferent way had also hated him.' But Nathan pleads with Caleb, as Starbuck did in vain with Ahab; and this plea is not in vain. Caleb cuts loose the dark canoe and they sail for home.

There is much in this short book: a surprising amount. It raises the difficult question whether a novel can depend upon another and still live in its own right. I am disposed to think that an author is as much entitled to draw upon a classic novel as upon myth; and *Moby Dick* as much as any novel has the size and depth of myth; the test, as I have suggested in discussing books based on myth, is whether the author has successfully absorbed his material and made it his own. By that test it must be said that *The Dark Canoe* fails. Though relevant parts of *Moby Dick* are explained, O'Dell's book does not fully live apart from Melville's; does not make full imaginative or psychological sense without it.

Sing Down the Moon (1970) is again a short book: too short perhaps for the story it has to tell. It is concerned with the sufferings of the Navajo Indians who were driven from their homes and forced into the long, dreadful march to Fort Sumner in 1864. The story is told in the first person by a young Navajo girl, Bright Morning; and, as in *Island of the Blue Dolphins,* O'Dell shows a gift for assuming a feminine identity which is all the more remarkable in a writer whose work is generally very masculine. There is a lovely, grave simplicity in this telling; yet one feels that perhaps it has been pared down too far, that a style which was admirably suited to the lonely setting of a Pacific island is less appropriate for a story that is full of people and harsh, clashing action. With the limpid brevity of *Sing Down the Moon* goes a sense of remoteness, almost of withdrawal.

Journey to Jericho (1969) is a story for younger children about David and the jar of watermelon pickle he takes with him when he travels from West Virginia to join his father in California. The jar, carefully cherished throughout the journey, falls into proportion (and on to the ground, and into fragments) when David sees his father and runs to his arms. It is a pleasant enough story, but the adjustment to a small child's eye level does not seem to come easily to this author. To write about real life for young children without being crabbed by the restricted range of a child's experience, one needs a particular lightness of touch, a gift for seeing ordinary things in a fresh, un-ordinary way which is childlike in a good sense of the word. This gift can be found in different forms in the work of Meindert DeJong and Eleanor Estes, and in the young children's books of William Mayne.

One suspects that a quick, light step is not natural to Scott O'Dell. His is a more measured tread. And probably he is a long-distance man. His most substantial books have been his most successful, and *The King's Fifth*—a sombre, almost stately novel—is his best of all. It must be significant, too, that he has found inspiration in that most massive of classics, *Moby Dick.* His best stories grow, moreover, from roots which are planted in known experience, actual places, historical fact, books; and there is neither wit nor humour in them. His imagination is strong but it does not soar or sparkle. He is a natural heavyweight.

Scott O'Dell wrote in the course of an article in PSYCHOLOGY TODAY in January 1968:

Books of mine which are classified officially as books for children were not written *for* children. Instead, and in a very real sense, they were written for myself. There is about all of them, however, one distinction which I feel is important to this form of literature: they were written consistently in the emotional area that children share with adults.

This area is much wider and much deeper than commonly it is supposed to be. Not that children are pocket editions of adults in the matter of feeling; nor do they react to the same stimuli as their elders. But they do have their own frustrations and hopes, a sense of the mystery that surrounds life, and a curiosity about it.

I believe that the child looks at the world with a sense of wonder. He wishes to know how it was fashioned and by whom. He wants to know why people behave as they do. He wants to know what it is to be good and truthful and fair, kind and courageous. Above all, he has the ability, which in adults either is eroded or entirely lost, to identify himself with the characters of a story.

Writing books for oneself, which hopefully children will read, has at least two motivations. It is an effort to placate whatever ghosts may persist, to make in the word of Sigmund Freud a 'poetical confession'. It also is an attempt, conscious or not, to work out through a form of self-analysis a needed and desired personal development.

Island of the Blue Dolphins began in anger, anger at the hunters who invade the mountains where I live and who slaughter everything that creeps or walks or flies. This anger also was directed at myself, at the young man of many years ago, who thoughtlessly committed the same crimes against nature . . .

I remember these depredations with horror. This horror,

muted but nonetheless real, colours the latter part of the book and the latter part only, because my Indian girl began her life, as most children do, in the closed world of selfishness where everything – whether clothed in fur or feathers – was an object of indifferent cruelty.

Through her I wished to say to the young and to all who wish to listen that we have a chance to come into a new relationship to the things around us. Once, in Defoe's day, we were cunning, manipulative children, living in a palace of nature. In her brief lifetime, she made the change from that world, where everything lived only to be exploited, into a humane and meaningful world . . .

With the publication of a book for adults, an author usually hears from most of his friends and none of his enemies. Afterwards there is silence. But with the children, if they like your book, the reverse is true. They respond in numbers, by the thousands of letters, over an indefinite period of time. It is this response and concern that to me make the work of an author worth the doing.

There are, of course, a few letters that you wish you had not received – the one from the boy in Minnesota, for example. Asked to write, as a class assignment, to the author of a book he recently had read, this youngster penned a long and dutiful letter, full of self-conscious compliments, and ended out-of-breath with this rather startling remark: 'Goodbye for now, you old jerk.'

And yet, of all the audiences, children are the finest!

Scott O'Dell

Bibliography

Books for children:

ISLAND OF THE BLUE DOLPHINS. Houghton Mifflin, 1960; Longman, 1961.
THE KING'S FIFTH. Houghton Mifflin, 1966; Longman, 1967.
THE BLACK PEARL. Houghton Mifflin, 1967; Longman, 1968.
THE DARK CANOE. Houghton Mifflin, 1968; Longman, 1969.
JOURNEY TO JERICHO. Houghton Mifflin, 1969.
SING DOWN THE MOON. Houghton Mifflin, 1970.

Philippa Pearce

Philippa Pearce was the youngest of four children of a flour-miller and corn-merchant at Great Shelford, Cambridgeshire. She was educated at the Perse Girls' School in Cambridge, and then at Girton College. For thirteen years, until 1958, she worked as a scriptwriter and producer in the School Broadcasting Department of the BBC, and for the next two years was an editor in the Educational Department of the Oxford University Press. From 1960 to 1967 she was children's editor for the publishing house of André Deutsch Ltd. Her books include Minnow on the Say *(1955),* Tom's Midnight Garden *(1958) which was awarded the Carnegie Medal,* Mrs Cockle's Cat *(1961),* A Dog So Small *(1962), and—in collaboration with Sir Brian Fairfax-Lucy—* The Children of the House *(1968).*

In 1965 I said, in *Written for Children*, that if I were asked to name a single masterpiece of English children's literature since the Second World War it would be *Tom's Midnight Garden*. One masterpiece in twenty years, I added, was a fair ration. Since 1965 some outstanding books have appeared in the children's lists. Restricting myself deliberately to England alone, I think at once of Mayne's *Earthfasts*, Garner's *The Owl Service*, Helen Cresswell's *The Piemakers*, K. M. Peyton's *Flambards*; and I think of Leon Garfield, who has seemed all through his brief career as a published writer to be on the point of producing a masterpiece. But 'masterpiece' is not a word to be lightly tossed around. Today I would still use it of only one book published since the last war, and the book would still be *Tom's Midnight Garden*. And one masterpiece in a quarter of a century is still a fair ration.

In a brief essay it seems best to be sparing in what is said about Philippa Pearce's other work. She is not, in fact, a prolific writer. She has published two other novels for children, *Minnow on the Say* (1955) and *A Dog So Small* (1962). She wrote the text of a picture-book, *Mrs Cockle's Cat* (1961), and reshaped a manuscript by Sir Brian Fairfax-Lucy to make *The Children of the House* (1968.) She has also written for radio and television, and has other, less substantial, work in print.

Minnow on the Say was Miss Pearce's first book, and a very attractive one. 'Minnow' is a canoe, and the Say is the river on which David Moss and his friend Adam Codling paddle her. And the title has an odd kind of aptness, for the action of the story is quick and light in relation to the slow depth of the setting. On the surface it is a neat treasure-hunt, with ingenious verse clues made still more ingenious by a transposition half way through which requires the same words to be differently interpreted. It is intellectually teasing and pleasing, and pretty much on the level of a good detective novel. The main characters are adequate but not specially interesting, apart perhaps from Adam, a boy in whom one senses already the man he is going to be. But surrounding and underlying it the rural community is strong and solid, and the river Say gives the book its distinctive feeling: suggesting, as a river will in the work of an artist who is fully conscious of it both as thing and as symbol, the changing course of life, the flow of time.

A Dog So Small is the story of a boy's longing for a dog. Ben Blewitt is the lonely middle child in a family of five. Grandpa Fitch promises him a dog for his birthday, but cannot keep the promise, and all Ben gets is an old picture of a dog worked in wool. And so he comes to imagine a dog of his own, a chihuahua, 'a dog so small that you can only see it with your eyes shut'. Watching it with eyes closed, Ben is run over in the street. He recovers and all ends well, for he gets his dog: not the marvellous animal of his imagination but an ordinary mongrel that he must learn to live with.

This is a homely story, with nothing rarefied or 'literary' about it. You might even say it is a bit ordinary; a child's longing for a pet is commonplace, but to explore the depths of this longing is not so common. (Meindert DeJong is one of the few other writers who have done it well.) As elsewhere, Philippa Pearce is perceptive about the relationships of young and old. Grandpa and Granny Fitch are the most rounded and satisfactory characters in the book: Grandpa has retired after many years in a humble job on the roads and is still fairly spry but definitely second in command; Granny, who brought up eight children in a hard-pressed, hardworking, successful life, has always made the decisions and has a proper sense of her own authority. The doggy parts of the book are excellent, too. When Grandpa Fitch's bitch Tilly is with her litter in the pigsty you can practically *smell* the puppies and feel them squirming under your hands.

Collaborations are difficult to assess as part of the work of one writer. A successful collaboration is a compound rather than a mixture and the contribution made by each partner can hardly be separated. *The Children of the House* is not exactly a novel: it is an account of Edwardian childhood which hovers on the borders of memory and imagination. The finished book bears the unmistakable stamp of Philippa Pearce; the material must be Sir Brian's, but the tale and telling are now one.

The book tells simply of the small adventures of four lonely children in the twilight years of a great house and estate. These are children whose parents have little time for them, whose clothes are not fit to wear, who long to be asked out to tea or given free sweets at the shop. The parents are not cruel, at least not intentionally, but they are uncomprehending; and they are preoccupied, worried, holding with difficulty to a way of life that slips away. Father is thrifty to the point of miserliness, at least when it comes to spending on his children; yet there is a full staff of servants, indoor and outdoor. And from the servants the children get the nearest thing in their lives to parental love and understanding. No present-day generation gap, no rift between parents and children could be greater than this one. At one point Papa and Mama go away for a couple of days and the children are left in the great hall, 'no longer a place for respectful steps and hushed voices'.

> 'Hurrah!' cried Laura, and 'Hurrah-rah-rah!' shouted Tom, running and leaping ahead of them all, beneath the gaze of those centuries of Stanfords; and 'Boo!' said Hugh, stopping abruptly to flap his arms beneath the portrait of Grandpapa Hatton, as if hoping to startle him from his godly expression; and Margaret jumped about with them and laughed till she was sobbing with over-excitement.

> The sun cast patterns of red, blue and yellow through the stained glass windows on to the family portraits, the busts, the suits of armour, and down on to the twirling figures of the children of the house dancing for joy over the marble floor.

These children are celebrating their parents' absence. It is a fearful as well as a vivid scene. The harshness of their bleak childhood is mitigated only by the comfort the children can draw from each other and from the pitying servants. And the parents' cold frugality is unavailing, for at last comes the First World War to break all up. The story is brought into touch with the present by brief prologue and epilogue. And in the end there is little left but the house; for three of the children have died in the war, and the youngest, poor Margaret, who is 'only ninepence in the shilling' mentally, cannot bear to live there. But 'the house', says the caretaker's wife, 'remembers'; and the reader will not soon forget.

Mrs Cockle's Cat is a collaboration of a different kind. Here the text is Philippa Pearce's, but the book as a whole is equally the product of Anthony Maitland, whose illustrations for it won the Library Association's Kate Greenaway medal. The area of pictures is indeed greater than that of text, and Maitland could claim to be, equally with Miss Pearce, the creator of Mrs Cockle (Cockney from hat to boots) and the handsome, faithless black cat Peter who loves fresh fish even more than he loves her company. The book has exactly the right picture-book mixture of real-life accuracy and wild invention.

And so to *Thom's Midnight Garden*, which is still Philippa Pearce's best book and still, to my mind, the best book that has ever won the Carnegie Medal. It could not, I think, be deduced from the rest of her work, for all its distinction, that she would write anything quite so good as this. The sense of place and atmosphere, the mastery over words, can be found in *Minnow on the Say* and elsewhere; but the full power of imagination, the perfect shaping, the ear for that particular strain of the still sad music of humanity which is also the music of time, belong only to *Tom's Midnight Garden*.

Tom himself is hardly 'a character': he is any child, any person.

He could be you. In quarantine for measles, he goes to stay with his loving, childless Aunt Gwen and with Uncle Alan who reads a clever weekly paper and is ready to reason with a child but hasn't the slightest understanding. They have a flat in a converted house owned by old Mrs Bartholomew, who lives at the top of it. The house has no garden – now. But Tom finds that at night he can slip out into the garden which used to belong to it in its late Victorian heyday. There he plays with a small girl named Hatty, who – unlike her family and the servants – can see him, though she thinks him a ghost. But although Tom's visits to the garden are taking place nightly in his own time, in Hatty's time they are at long intervals; she begins to grow up, to grow beyond him. At the end of the story, when Tom is about to leave for home, he meets old Mrs Bartholomew and realizes that she is Hatty; night by night she has been dreaming of her past life as a lonely child, and lonely Tom has been able to enter it with her.

If I understand it correctly, the book is concerned with the four-dimensional wholeness of life. In the child the old person is implicit; in the old person the child remains. There are clues. At the end, Aunt Gwen says that 'of course, Mrs Bartholomew's such a shrunken little old woman, she's hardly bigger than Tom, anyway: but, you know, he put his arms right round her and he hugged her good-bye as if she were a little girl'. And, just before, Tom has been talking to Mrs Bartholomew about their encounters as children, so long ago and at the same time so recent. 'We're both real; Then and Now,' he says; and he quotes the angel from the Book of Revelation who declared that there should be Time No Longer. Time No Longer, or Time All One; it is the same thing. Books are sometimes said, in a phrase of stereotyped approval, to have an extra dimension. Of *Tom's Midnight Garden* this is no cliché.

There have been many, many time fantasies. Few have had so precise a formal structure, but that would not in itself make *Tom's Midnight Garden* so excellent a novel. There is a profundity of thought and feeling here that goes far deeper than the exposition of a mathematical theory. Successive phases of life, especially the transition from childhood to maturity, are shown symbolically. Philippa Pearce herself has said (in *Chosen for Children*, the Library Association book on the Carnegie medal-winners) that the walled garden represents the sheltered security of early childhood; but Tom climbs the high garden wall and describes to Hatty the extensive and tempting view – of adult life – beyond. Later Hatty, now a young woman, skates along the frozen river to Ely, where she climbs the tower of the Cathedral; and on the way back she meets the young man Barty and sees Tom no more. She has outgrown him.

If both Then and Now are to be real, we must believe in Then. And we do; for Then is every bit as real as the dustbin-crowded back area and surrounding sea of suburbia that beset the house Now. In Tom's successive visits to the garden – at first exploring it by himself, then encountering people, and later venturing beyond its bounds – the story quietly takes possession of the past. But in terms of our own perception even the past appears to move. As a symbol of childhood a garden is not static, for in the beauty of any garden is an evanescent sensuousness; today is not as yesterday and tomorrow will not be as today; the season moves on.

A novel for children should, in my view, 'work' at surface level; and *Tom's Midnight Garden* does. The page cries out to be turned; the reader wants to know what happens next; the ending satisfactorily rounds off the story. But there are also echoes and resonances, beauties and mysteries that I believe every reader will be conscious of but none will fully grasp. And at each return to the book the search for what remains elusive can be renewed. *Tom's Midnight Garden* is not a book to be grown out of. I have read it several times and still find it continually rewarding. It is not cosy or jolly; there is nothing to laugh out loud over; but there is joy in it: the joy that is just this side of sadness.

Philippa Pearce writes:

As a child, I intended to be a writer – a novelist, of course. It's a common dream. The nearest I seemed likely to get, as an adult, was in the job of scriptwriter-producer for the School Broadcasting Department of the BBC. This experience, over thirteen years, must have helped as much as any to make me into a writer of children's books. I wrote for the same public, changing only the medium.

In scriptwriting I learned professionalism: to write to a certain length; to cut, and – more basically – to be *prepared* to cut; to achieve a beginning, a middle, and an end without being a bore about it; and so on. Many of our scripts were literary adaptations, and then one had to understand the structure and workings of a story before beginning to select and dramatize. Above all, I was learning to write directly for speaking. Clearly this relates itself to the great oral tradition of story-telling for children.

In 1951, while I was working for school broadcasting, I contracted tuberculosis. I went into hospital in Cambridge for most of that summer, a particularly fine one. I didn't feel ill at all, and it seemed almost unbearable to be lying in bed missing all of the summer on the river, only five miles away, in Great Shelford, where I had been born and brought up. My parents were then still living in the Mill House, with the river flowing by the garden. Imprisoned in hospital, I went there in my imagination as I had never done before – as I had never needed to do, of course. I knew, by heart, literally the *feel* of the river and the canoe on it. It became hallucinatory, like vividly-imagined fiction.

At last I went back to work; but now began to dawn on me the idea that I could do it too – write a children's story. One needed a good, reliable plot, of course: a search for treasure; a family home on its last legs; and so on. As for the setting, I had that already; and that was what really interested me.

I wrote *Minnow on the Say* mostly with pleasure. I was just about to let the heroes find their treasure (at a point half way through what is now the finished story) when I realized that the whole thing would be on the short side. So, with a dislocating wrench, I changed the plot: the treasure wasn't there, after all, and the characters had to plod on through renewed complications.

About the time that *Minnow on the Say* was published, my parents sold the Mill House. My father had already retired from milling, and his mill – like all, or nearly all, small country mills – ceased working for good. The Mill House had become too big, with its seven bedrooms and its splendidly-proportioned but unheatable rooms downstairs. Ah, but it was a thoroughly *nice* house, in the way some people are nice! You see such houses all over East Anglia still. It's exactly the house of *Tom's Midnight Garden*, with a storey added for Mrs Bartholomew; its garden is – or was – almost exactly that garden.

I began to think out *Tom*. At first, in reaction against the first book, this one was to have had a minimum of plot; but, of course, it changed and grew. At least it has more of a theme than a plot. I still think it the best of the books I have written: I think it's the best done, and it's the closest, dearest.

I used to think – and to say in print – that authors of children's books usually wrote out of childhood experience: that I myself certainly did. Now I'm not sure; almost, I'm sure not. That is, I think I write out of present experience; but present experience includes – sometimes painfully – the past.

Philippa Pearce

Bibliography

MINNOW ON THE SAY. Oxford University Press, 1955; World, 1958, as MINNOW LEADS TO TREASURE.

TOM'S MIDNIGHT GARDEN. Oxford University Press, 1958; Lippincott, 1959.

MRS COCKLE'S CAT. Longman, 1961; Lippincott, 1963.

A DOG SO SMALL. Longman, 1962; Lippincott, 1963.

FROM INSIDE SCOTLAND YARD (with Harold Scott). André Deutsch, 1963; Macmillan, 1965.

THE STRANGE SUNFLOWER. Nelson, London, 1966.

THE CHILDREN OF THE HOUSE (with Brian Fairfax-Lucy). Longman, 1968; Lippincott, 1968.

THE ELM STREET LOT. B.B.C. Publications (*Jackanory series*), 1969.

Short stories for children by Philippa Pearce include *Still Jim and Silent Jim* in ANOTHER SIX (Blackwell, 1959) and *Return to Air* in THE FRIDAY MIRACLE AND OTHER STORIES, edited by Kaye Webb (Puffin Books, 1969).

K. M. Peyton

Kathleen Peyton was born in 1929. She went to Wimbledon High School, then to art school at Kingston-on-Thames and Manchester, and ran away from home to marry her husband Michael, a freelance commercial artist. During the next few years she travelled to many parts of the world and held a variety of jobs. Her first published book— Sabre, The Horse from the Sea*—had been written when she was fifteen, and was followed by two other horse novels and four adventure stories for boys. In 1963,* Windfall *was published by Oxford University Press, to be followed by* The Maplin Bird *(1964),* The Plan for Birdsmarsh *(1965),* Thunder in the Sky *(1966),* Flambards *(1967),* Fly-By-Night *(1968), and* The Edge of the Cloud *and* Flambards in Summer *(1969). Four of her books were runners-up for the Carnegie Medal before she finally won it with* The Edge of the Cloud. *The trilogy consisting of this and the two Flambards books received the 1970* Guardian *award.*

Mrs Peyton and her husband have two daughters and live in Essex.

Strictly speaking, there is no such person as K. M. Peyton. There is Kathleen Peyton, who has written several books; and there is Michael, her husband, who collaborated in some of the earlier ones. A former publisher did not like the look of 'by K.and M. Peyton' on a jacket or title-page, and so K. M. Peyton was born. But today 'K. M. Peyton' means Kathleen.

Mrs Peyton had in fact written her first published novel when she was Kathleen Herald, aged fifteen and even before that she had produced half a dozen unpublished manuscripts, spread over many exercise books. 'I have always had a book on the go since the age of nine,' she once said. She married at twenty-one and spent much of the next few years travelling widely and impecuniously with her husband. By the time she was thirty-two she had published three novels about horses, four adventure stories for boys which first appeared as serials in *Scout* magazine, and much miscellaneous material, including the ghosted memoirs of a dog-trainer. Then, deciding she could afford to write a book to please herself, she produced *Windfall*, a story of sea adventure which was somewhat longer and a good deal deeper than her earlier ones. Its publication by Oxford University Press in 1963 marked her immediate breakthrough to the front rank of 'quality' children's writers.

Since then, Mrs Peyton has steadily increased her range. I have seen it suggested that she has developed her true self as a writer by moving away from *Windfall*, but I do not agree. *Windfall* was the work of a mature person and experienced writer, and has many of the best Peyton qualities. The K. M. Peyton of today includes the author of *Windfall*, and indeed of the earlier books. She is a person of action, and a writer on themes of action. She has, among many other gifts, the unusual one of writing extremely well about *movement*: about the way people move with and through and against the elements, in boats, on horseback, and—in the *Flambards* novels—in those frail, wind-buffeted early aircraft.

The storytelling and command of material in *Windfall* are superb. It is clear from every page that the author knew from her own perilous experience what it was like to sail a fishing smack in winter off the Essex shores, as her hero Matt does in that book. First-class adventure stories are not too common today, and ones as good as *Windfall* are rare indeed. The surge and swell of the story are almost enough to make a reader seasick. The villain, Beckett, has been criticized as being a figure of unqualified evil, but this criticism seems to me mistaken. Stories of peril at sea call for elemental qualities in their human participants, as many awesome precedents remind us. The psychological subtleties of the drawing-room are inappropriate when the ship is listing at forty-five degrees, the sea sweeping the decks, the hull all but invisible, the mizzen-mast gone, and the rigging trailing in the sea 'like the hair of a drowning woman'.

But although a splendid story, *Windfall* is clearly pressing against the confines of its genre. Matt is a figure of what the author herself calls 'simple courage', entirely right for the hero of a sea story; yet she shows him in a longer perspective, as a lad assuming adult responsibility, as a member of a community, and in his relationship with the rich man's son, Francis. The nature and limitation of this relationship are accurately summed up in the closing chapter, in which both boys realize that a temporary friendship has run its course and that their ways have to part. The next step seems—with benefit of hindsight—obvious: that the author should add to her next book the further dimensions of depth of character and social analysis. And Mrs Peyton did indeed move in this direction with *The Maplin Bird* (1964), a story about an orphaned brother and sister in mid-Victorian England, in which the sea and fishing-smacks again play an important but less dominant rôle. *The Maplin Bird* also marks the appearance of the first heroine in Mrs Peyton's mature work. Matt in *Windfall* had a sister, Anne, who barely had a speaking part; but Emily in *The Maplin Bird* steals the story entirely from her brother Toby. She is resourceful, spirited, enduring; and she matures in the course of the action, as Mrs Peyton's heroes generally do not. *The Maplin Bird* has a limited happy ending; Emily's love for the gentleman-smuggler Adam Seymour brings her only pain, but she and brother Toby finish up with a cottage of their own, and freedom.

The Plan for Birdsmarsh (1965) and *Fly-by-Night* (1968) are Mrs Peyton's only stories, up to the time of writing, with contemporary settings. Birdsmarsh is a sleepy Essex village faced with the threat (or promise, depending on one's point of view) of development with a marina, hotel, swimming-pool, giant car-park and the rest. Dreamy, un-boaty Paul hates the thought of it, but his friend Gus, a local working lad, can see the advantages. The resulting story is interwoven with a virtually separate one about a lifesaving suit invented by Paul's elder brother Chris and the trapping of a pair of industrial spies. The difficulty is not merely one of working two plots together: it is that the two plots belong to different kinds of book, an exploration of personal and social conflicts and an adventure story. The natural pace and the kinds of character required are not the same for both types of story. The result, to my mind, is an interesting failure, although the author has again extended her range, and Paul is more subtle than any of her previous heroes. *Fly-by-Night* is quite slight, a horsy story, successfully fulfilling a limited aim, and returning to some of the same themes as the author's very first book. In each is a girl with the single-minded aim of owning a horse, and each girl achieves the aim with very little outside help. In *Sabre*, written when Mrs Peyton was in her teens, the appearance of a horse from the sea has a mysterious, almost mystical aspect, and there are elements of the wildest wish-fulfilment. *Fly-by-Night*, twenty years later, is a great deal more down-to-earth. Liza in *Sabre* and Ruth in *Fly-by-Night* are minor Peyton heroines but unmistakable: determined and somewhat formidable.

Thunder in the Sky (1966) went back in time to the start of the First World War, but was a big advance on *The Plan for Birdsmarsh* the previous year. While the latter is a complicated and somewhat uncoordinated story, *Thunder in the Sky* has a more rewarding kind of complexity. It can be read at more than one level. Sam Goodchild, at fifteen, works on the coastal sailing barges which have been switched at the start of the war to carrying freight and later ammunition to France. He cannot understand why his elder brother Gil, also on the barges, doesn't join the Army like any other young man. There is espionage in the air, and it looks as if Gil might be involved. Sam eavesdrops in a Calais bar, is caught, tied up, released, pursued out to sea, fired on; and so it continues until the climax in which Gil, who was indeed passing messages to the other side, sails his barge, loaded with explosives and on fire from a Zeppelin raid, away from the pier to a death that atones for everything.

At its face value this is what used to be called a rattling good yarn; and none the worse for that. Yet a reader who has passed beyond the stage of reading simply for plot and action will also find himself engaged with themes of the morality and pity of war, and with the ambiguous character of brother Gil. At the more mature level I do not think the book is entirely satisfactory. At this level it may appear that Gil is the true centre of interest rather than honest, innocent Sam, who is something of a throwback to the earlier brave but simple Peyton heroes. And one wants to know more about Gil; to see more of the background to his non-enlistment, his involvement in espionage, his suffering. We learn that he needs money to spend on a girl, and this may be explanation enough for younger readers, but, to cast a shadow of such length, Gil's love affair with faithless Agnes must be more than a mere plotting device. The author knows this and hints at it:

> When Gil had got enough rum inside him, he called for Agnes Martin. George Young came to the door and told him to clear off, but Gil seized him by the collar of his smart white shirt, pulled him into the road and hit him. Agnes came out, saw George rolling in the dust and laughed. Then Gil told her to get her coat, and they went down the lane, their arms round each other, to where the tide was making silently over the shining mud, and the waders cried along the sea-wall.

We get only a glimpse or two of Agnes; she belongs to the 'other' book that the author did not write and probably never thought of writing, but that one feels to be present in a ghostly way behind *Thunder in the Sky*.

It is easy to suggest that the same book should 'work at all levels'; it is not easy and may often be impossible to meet this exacting demand. But the trilogy which began with *Flambards* in 1967 is complete and rounded-out while *Thunder in the Sky*, for all its merits, is not. Of all Kathleen Peyton's work, this trilogy seems to me to be the most satisfying as well as the most substantial.

Flambards is the name of the decrepit country house to which the heroine Christina is sent at the start of the first book to live with her crippled, violent Uncle Russell and his two sons. The family fortunes, undermined by Uncle's expensive passion for horses and hunting, are in a desperate state; and Christina, who will be rich when she comes of age, suspects that she is meant to restore them by marrying Mark, the elder son. Mark, handsome and arrogant, shares his father's obsession with hunting. Will, the gentle younger brother, hates and fears riding and longs to fly aeroplanes, those flimsy, precarious things that are just starting to rise above the hedgerows. Then there is Dick, the groom, who teaches Christina to ride, and is kinder than anyone. All three love Christina in their various ways; but it is Will, the pioneer aviator, who carries her off from the dying house in the first book's final chapter.

The changing relationships of people are seen within a framework which is itself changing: sinking squirearchy and rising technocracy, old and new attitudes, class barriers that are still strong but showing the first cracks. It is a book of conflicts, extending right into the personality of the heroine, for Christina has something of the hard-riding Russells in herself, even though in the end she makes her firm choice of new against old, person against place or position, the gentle against the ruthless. It is a book of action in the exterior sense, too: there are vivid scenes of hunting, of early motoring and flying, of personal violence. (Uncle Russell's beating of William for disobedience and Dick's beating-up of Mark for making his sister pregnant are both disturbingly powerful.) A novel will no more live through structure alone than a body through having a skeleton; both need flesh and blood as well, and *Flambards* has them.

The second and third books of the trilogy – *The Edge of the Cloud* and *Flambards in Summer*, both published in 1969 – satisfactorily complete the design, although they do not add to the stature which *Flambards* has established. The former deals largely with Will's career as an aviator in the years immediately before the First World War. It is seen from the point of view of Christina, who fears for him with good cause, and suffers daily on his behalf. As a book on its own, *The Edge of the Cloud* is concerned with the tensions of a relationship overshadowed by danger and by a sense of impermanence; it deals, too, with the further tensions that arise where the young man's first love is for his vocation but the young woman's love is all for *him*. It stands somewhat apart from the other two books of the trilogy, which are centred on the house itself.

Possibly, indeed, the Flambards saga is really a two-part story, with the middle book as a prolonged interlude. In the third book we are back at Flambards. Uncle Russell has died; Will has been killed in the war and his brother Mark is reported missing. Christina, who has now come into her money, returns to the run-down house to pick up the pieces, to bear Will's posthumous child, to work the home farm. 'Flambards,' she has said to the house near the end of the first book, 'you are dying.' The theme of *Flambards in Summer* is rebirth, not only of the house but of the little community that belongs to it and that now takes a new form. And it is Christina who gives life, in all senses of the phrase. She is a heroine on the grand scale for a modern novel: determined, undaunted and above all strong – stronger by far than the men in her life.

Mrs Peyton has her limitations as a novelist. Some are straightforward limitations of scope and subject-matter such as all writers must have. She has not yet written a work of fantasy or humour, and no young child has a speaking part in any of her books except *Flambards in Summer*, where Mark's son Tizzy appears but is seen from an adult viewpoint. Her characters are mainly people of action, and even the gentle individualists like Will in the Flambards novels and Paul in *Birdsmarsh* show little sign of having any literary or artistic interests. Of her masculine characters, some – like Matt in *Windfall*, Sam in *Thunder in the Sky* and Dick in the Flambards books – are simple, brave, and slightly wooden; others, like the gentleman smuggler Adam in *The Maplin Bird* and the handsome cad Mark in *Flambards*, strike one as being related to the creations of feminine romantic novelists. Her two splendid heroines, Emily and Christina, are, as she says herself, 'more or less the same person'; and both of them, even in their teens, are women, not girls. The last thing a Peyton heroine would ever be is girlish.

But Mrs Peyton can deal with large themes, and construct excellent plots if she is so minded. She can tell a story with great pace and certainty. In her historical, or semi-historical, novels her research appears impeccable, but she never gives the impression of bookishness; she knows in her fingers how to handle a boat or a horse, and one feels she would manage quite well in an ancient aeroplane. She has extended her territory book by book, and undoubtedly will extend it further. And there is one vital moment that occurs sooner or later in most of her novels and accounts for much of their depth and strength: the moment of rejoicing at simply being here, to love and suffer and take what comes.

K. M. Peyton writes:

I do not base my characters on actual people. I generally know them fairly well before I start to write, as I always have my next book, or even my next two, in my head when I am writing the current one. I think about them a lot, I suppose, while doing things like painting (boats or walls, not pictures). I generally plot from the beginning and the end inwards, usually having a lot of trouble about the three-quarter-way mark. The end I usually know before anything.

I used to consider 700 words an average day and 1,000 pretty good, but now write more quickly than I did, and do 3,000 on a really good day. I wrote *The Edge of the Cloud* in three months, but took over a year with *Windfall*. I like to do the research for a book, and read books relevant to the period all the time. I enjoy this part of it, even going to Beckton gasworks for *Thunder in the Sky* and the Admiralty's hydrographical centre for the buoyage of the Thames estuary for *The Maplin Bird*. Often research on one book will set me off on the next—for example, researching the tiny bit in *Thunder in the Sky* about the aeroplane that rescued the barge when it was being fired on by the Frenchman set me off on the flying theme in *Flambards*.

I think my two heroines Emily and Christina are more or less the same person, and both rather untypical of the period I set them in. Everything Emily suffered in the smack 'My Alice' in *The Maplin Bird* I had suffered in my own sailing experience at this time. *The Plan for Birdsmarsh* had more or less a ready-made plot, in that the survival-suit idea was real and we had been helping the inventor, a friend of ours, to test it from our own boat. Michael, who did and still does the drawings for the *New Scientist*, had all the information on industrial spies, and the marina plan was being splashed in the local newspaper, so I put it all together, the various themes getting rather out of control at times, I feel.

Thunder in the Sky took more work than any of my other books, a great deal of research being required. Where we live is still the home of the remaining sailing barges, and there are quite a lot of the old skippers still around to talk about their experiences. I knew absolutely nothing about the 1914–18 war when I started this book. I think seeing Joan Littlewood's production of *Oh, What a Lovely War!* probably started me off on this subject; I don't think I have been so moved by anything as by that play. Books that also opened my eyes were Robert Graves's *Goodbye to All That*, Frank Richards's *Old Soldiers Never Die*, and, most of all, Siegfried Sassoon's books. (I think *Memoirs of a Fox-Hunting Man* is my idea of a perfect book.) I knew what the general theme of *Thunder in the Sky* was going to be, and had the setpiece of sailing out the burning ammunition barge in my mind in all its detail before I worked out the plot. I like Gil one of the best of all my characters. I remember I wrote all that part in a great frenzy and blew him up on Christmas Eve, and then had to do the sprouts and mince pies and fill the children's stockings, and I was in a complete daze all the time.

When I came to *Flambards*, I was tired of writing about sailing and decided to have a complete change. I enjoyed writing this book, and particularly its successor, more than any I have written. I have always loved aeroplanes, and during the Second World War could recognize them all, so I thoroughly enjoyed all the reading-up involved. I did not write *Flambards* with the intention of having a sequel, but the idea developed and I could see two more books eventually. *Fly-by-Night* I wrote for a rest, and because the girls wanted a pony book; also because I thought it would be a good idea to do a book that I could illustrate myself. I had bought an unbroken New Forest pony and broken him in, and as, like Ruth, I didn't know much about it, the story is virtually that of our own experience with Cracker.

I write exactly what I want to write, and since it appears to have found an appreciative market I feel I am very lucky. I think I must be a compulsive writer. The only time I never had any ideas or cared about it at all was when I was pregnant.

K. M. Peyton

Bibliography

SABRE, THE HORSE FROM THE SEA (under the name Kathleen Herald). A. and C. Black, 1947; Macmillan, New York, 1963.
THE MANDRAKE (under the name Kathleen Herald). A. and C. Black, 1949.
CRAB THE ROAN (under the name Kathleen Herald). A. and C. Black, 1953.
NORTH TO ADVENTURE. Collins, 1959; Platt and Munk, 1965.
STORMCOCK MEETS TROUBLE. Collins, 1961.
THE HARD WAY HOME. Collins, 1962.
WINDFALL. Oxford University Press, 1963; World, 1963, as SEA FEVER.
BROWNSEA SILVER. Collins, 1964.
THE MAPLIN BIRD. Oxford University Press, 1964; World, 1965.
THE PLAN FOR BIRDSMARSH. Oxford University Press, 1965; World, 1966.
THUNDER IN THE SKY. Oxford University Press, 1966; World, 1967.
FLAMBARDS. Oxford University Press, 1967; World, 1968.
FLY-BY-NIGHT. Oxford University Press, 1968; World, 1969.
THE EDGE OF THE CLOUD. Oxford University Press, 1969; World, 1969.
FLAMBARDS IN SUMMER. Oxford University Press, 1969; World, 1970.
PENNINGTON'S SEVENTEENTH SUMMER. Oxford University Press, 1970; Thomas Y. Crowell, 1971, as PENNINGTON'S LAST TERM.

Short stories by K. M. Peyton include *A Man and a Boy* in MISCELLANY THREE, edited by Edward Blishen (Oxford University Press, 1966) and *The Day of the Fête* in THRILLING STORIES FROM THE PAST FOR GIRLS, edited by Eric Duthie (Odhams Press, 1969).

Ivan Southall

Ivan Southall was born in Melbourne in 1921. His early ambition was to be a journalist, and his first articles and short stories were published when he was sixteen. In the Second World War he became a pilot in the Royal Australian Air Force and eventually captained a Sunderland flying-boat. He was awarded the Distinguished Flying Cross for an action in which a U-boat was destroyed. After the war he spent two years in London, working on an official war history, and then returned to Australia to become a freelance writer. He is married and has four children.

Among his books for young readers are Hills End *(1962),* Ash Road *(1965),* To The Wild Sky *(1967), and* Chinaman's Reef Is Ours *(1970). Both* Ash Road *and* To The Wild Sky *were chosen as Australian Children's Books of the Year. He has also written many books for adults, including three well-known war books,* They Shall Not Pass Unseen, Bluey Truscott, *and* Softly Tread the Brave.

For more than a decade Ivan Southall wrote wholesome adventure stories about Squadron Leader Simon Black of the Royal Australian Air Force. Simon, according to an article by his creator in the *Horn Book* for June 1968, 'possessed in incredible measure virtue, honour, righteous anger, courage and inventiveness', as well as 'a very stiff upper lip'. The day came, as Southall said in that article (an extract from which follows this essay), when the thought of writing one more word about his super-hero was more than he could stomach. So Simon Black was bowler-hatted. Instead, Southall sat down and wrote a novel about a group of ordinary, unheroic, flesh-and-blood children of the kind he himself knew. Cut off by storm and flood in a little town in the mountains, miles from anywhere, with no parents around, these children faced catastrophe not with the aplomb of a fictional Air Force officer but with a lifelike mixture of bravery and cowardice, sense and silliness, co-operation and confusion. And, precariously but credibly, they blundered through. The book was *Hills End*, published in 1962. It was immediately successful in the United States and Britain as well as Australia. This book, and its successor *Ash Road*, began a new phase in Ivan Southall's career.

Surprisingly, it seemed by 1970 that Southall had not entirely discarded the support of a tried formula. His four full-length novels for children since *Hills End* have had strong similarities with that book and with each other. *Ash Road*, *To the Wild Sky* (1967), *Finn's Folly* (1969) and *Chinaman's Reef is Ours* (1970) have all been about groups of youngsters faced with disasters which tax their reserves of physical and moral courage to the utmost. A reader acquainted with, say, any two of these five books would have little difficulty in attributing the other three to Southall, even if he had nothing to go on but a plot summary. It is possible to feel that the author has repeated himself, and has sometimes piled on the horror in an effort to combat the law of diminishing returns. A parody of Southall could be written under the title of *Tether's End*. Yet each successive book has explored some new ground, and each has its own interest.

All five novels are cinematic in technique: the point of view roves around, cameralike, from one character or pair of characters to another. It is difficult to use this method effectively when the end-product is to be a book rather than a film, because, for most people, reading is not as compulsive as watching; the attention is jolted when the narrative jumps from one character to another, with the risk of loss of interest. It also requires a more-or-less equal build-up of a number of characters. Southall's ability to manage a large cast, and to make a number of children all interesting and all entirely different, is exceptional. In his plots, the major element is the catastrophe itself; storm and flood in *Hills End*, bush fire in *Ash Road*, air crash in *To the Wild Sky*, road accident in *Finn's Folly*, invasion of town by mining company in *Chinaman's Reef is Ours*. The catastrophe is foreshadowed early in the story—in *Hills End*, as early as the first sentence—and build-up of tension takes the place of surprise. In *Hills End* there is minor action—the quest for the cave paintings—to keep the story going until calamity strikes.

Hills End is almost a perfect novel of its kind. Although only one adult can be said to play a major rôle, the feeling of the whole community, adults as well as children, is strong from the start, as indeed it must be in order to give full weight to the blow that falls upon it. The rapid character development and self-discovery of the children under stress are notable. For instance, in a few days and a couple of hundred pages Adrian, the boss's son and 'king of the kids', discovers himself to be a physical coward and moves through deep self-disgust to find himself again as a resourceful organizer; and all this time he remains unmistakably the same boy. In *Ash Road* the scope is broader, a full cast of adults is introduced, and the account of the bush fire's progress is absorbing in itself; yet the fire is a long, long time in arriving, and the tension has to be sustained through many anticipatory chapters. Already there is a feeling that the author is straining to keep it up, that the characters are running around in too many circles. When Old Man George has a stroke, apparently through overwork and the heat of the day rather than anything to do with the fire, and when this is followed by panic-stricken and unsuccessful attempts to get him into hospital, one begins to wonder whether troubles have been multiplied unduly. *Ash Road*, to my mind, confirmed the achievement of *Hills End*, and showed that it was no flash-in-the-pan, but did not greatly add to it.

To the Wild Sky is a problem novel: the most remarkable and baffling of all Southall's books. Six children set off in a private plane on a weekend visit. The pilot dies suddenly of a heart attack and one of the boys manages to fly the machine but is prevented by dust-storms from trying to land it until many hours later when, carried by tail-winds for hundreds of miles beyond his destination, he makes a crash-landing on a remote shore. For the rest of the book the children are seeking in a disorganized way to survive; they have at the end the slight encouragement of making fire, but they have no water and virtually no food, and they have found no signs of current human life. We do not know what happens to them.

It seems to me that this book presents the first two acts of a three-act drama. The first act is the flight and the second is the children's stranding and their attempt to sort themselves out.

But what of the final act? Is it rescue, or is it – as seen in a premonition by one of the girls – death, slow and dreadful, one at a time? The author has left the last act to be written in the mind of the reader and the few clues he offers are, to my mind, indecisive. But is it legitimate, artistically, to leave the story to be finished by the reader? I do not think it is. To one reader at least it seems that the story is the author's, and that nobody else can say what happens. It is no longer axiomatic that a novel must have a beginning, a middle and an end, but I still believe it is not complete until all that *needs* telling has been told. In this case the significance of the first two acts depends to a large extent on the third. If the children are doomed, they are not the same children as if they survive; the meaning of the story, and of their lives, is different. The ambiguity is too profound to be left unresolved. This seems to me to be the real difficulty of *To the Wild Sky*. Comparisons with William Golding's *Lord of the Flies* are of little relevance. The point of *Lord of the Flies*, as I understand it, is that the castaway boys regress towards savagery. That does not happen in *To the Wild Sky*; in fact part of the problem faced by these children is that they are too civilized to cope.

Finn's Folly is an equally disturbing book. A crash at night on a hairpin bend in frost and fog; the parents of four children dead in their car; the driver of a lorry dying in his cab with his young daughter beside him; drums of deadly cyanide strewn around a hillside with a reservoir below; a mentally-retarded boy at large, and somewhere in the background the curse of a disastrous marriage still working itself out: it is hard to imagine a more harrowing set of circumstances. At the heart of the story is the brief love that springs up between fifteen-year-old Max and fourteen-year-old Alison, both just orphaned. Alison is still trapped in the cab of the truck beside her dead father.

> There was a soft laugh, unlike any other he had ever heard, and he knew that it was a very special sound: the first laugh of a girl for a boy. It could never happen again, not the same sound or the same excitement that it stirred. He laughed also, as quietly as she had, and said 'Gee, Alison . . . ' He went quiet then and was confused.

It is unlikely that a boy and girl would talk love in the midst of death and continuing crisis, but it is not impossible, for human nature is infinitely strange. And it is possible that their talk of love in these circumstances would not be callous or offensive. It seems that girl and boy are taking the places of lost mother and lost father for each other; and it could be that there is a deeper significance still, for here at the moment of death is the rebirth of love. If the author can make the incident credible in fact and acceptable in feeling, then objections must be withdrawn. But that is an exceedingly difficult task. I do not think it is accomplished. The explanation, perhaps, is that one feels oneself under pressure from the author; he is forcing a confrontation, issuing a challenge. And the pile-up of agony has been too great; the paradox is too extreme and deliberate. The power of belief will not stretch far enough and, in the absence of belief, the question of moral and emotional acceptability does not arise.

The action of *Finn's Folly* takes place within a night, and that of *Chinaman's Reef is Ours* within a day. A handful of families in an almost-ghost town 'built beside a copper-mine out in the middle of nowhere, Australia' faces the sudden arrival of 'a mammoth convoy of prime movers, trailers, bulldozers, caravans—all the might of the Pan Pacific Mining Company advancing like an invading army'. The company has bought up the town's leases and intends to demolish it and dig out what still lies underneath. The main characters are four local teenagers, their parents, and the man who heads the mining company's operation. With the invasion comes first a shattering eruption of all the issues that have stayed buried in the sanded-up life of the little community; then a panic in which everyone seems to be at cross-purposes; then the clash of attackers and attacked. The men drive off to seek support from the shire authorities, so it is the women and children who bear the heat of the day. And at the end of it all, the invaders prevail.

There is a lack of literal probability in this story. It is hard to believe that an invading force could or would be sent without warning one Sunday morning to destroy a town and make its people homeless. This seems the kind of conflict to stretch over weeks or months rather than to be fought and finished in a day. The air is one of confusion and over-wroughtness, as if everything had been artificially whipped up into this one brief flurry; as if the author had tried to give human catastrophe the character of a natural catastrophe, which – in peacetime and in what is largely a legal question – it does not possess.

Yet human conflict has possibilities which do not exist in fire or flood, in air or road crash. There is no arguing with *those*. The situation in *Chinaman's Reef* has its universal aspect – the quiet backwater finding itself in the way of material progress – and at one moment there is a glimpse of that progress in a horrifying, almost science-fictional aspect:

> Cherry drooped at her mother's window, looking out on a shuddering world where not a man moved on foot, where there was not a human face except behind windscreen glass. There they presided, dimly seen, not like living men, but like figures of wax that might eerily stir on command. Cherry leaned there and cried a little and felt a million years alone. Vehicles obstructed her view but allowed anguished glimpses of a yellow-painted monster nervily squirting black puffs of smoke and thrusting itself about in jerks and stabs in an ill-tempered way, each thrust bearing behind it thirty tons of steel.

For all its faults, this is a searching novel. Maybe the invaders have a point, and this 'heap of sticks and stones' doesn't deserve to stay – or has it a character, a shabby dignity, that should save it? And maybe it's not so bad for the men (who lack the initiative to compete elsewhere) or for the children (who will grow up and probably leave anyway) but isn't Chinaman's Reef a waste of life for the women? So says Cherry's mother, who – like Cherry herself, the teenager who minces her hips 'like a cheap little hussy' – emerges from the fight with some dignity. The people are all alive, and, as always, Southall is wonderfully good at showing the individual in action in a social context. But the chessboard technique, in which the pieces are moved forward separately yet all in concert with each other, does not really work here, because there is not a clear enough pattern to the action. The town's aged dowager, Auntie Sadie, built up strongly at the beginning, plays no effective part; the queen, as it were, moves to an isolated square at the start of the game and stays there.

Though the full-length novels carry more weight, two books which are closer to being long short stories seem to me to be among Southall's most successful work for children. These are *The Fox Hole* (1967) and *Let the Balloon Go* (1968.) In *The Fox Hole*, a boy called Ken is trapped in a shaft which may be that of a long-lost gold mine, and his uncle, setting out to rescue him, is deflected by the prospect of sudden wealth. This book's approach to the sinister lure of gold recalls Scott O'Dell's *The King's Fifth*, and is a reminder by contrast of the moral absence-of-mind which characterizes so many fictional treasure-hunts. *Let the Balloon Go* is a terse, memorable tale about a spastic boy inside whom an active, adventurous one is signalling desperately to get out. Reluctantly left at home for once by his anxious mother, John climbs to the top of an eighty-foot tree.

> It was everything he had longed for and never known. All words fell away, all demands that others should see him meant nothing any more. The bough swayed and he swayed with it; wind was like a cool sea against him; motion and wind together were a great calm that healed every pain he had ever known.
>
> He was strong. He was free. He was a boy like any other boy.

All that remains – but it is a nightmare for the neighbourhood – is that John should get safely down again.

'A balloon is not a balloon until you cut the string and let it go'; that is what the book is about. John's parents have done him no service by their over-protectiveness. This, and aspects of some other books, have caused Ivan Southall to be criticized for devaluing parents. Such criticisms, I feel, are unjustified. Southall, like other contemporary writers for children, has shown parents as fallible; he has not put them on the old pedestal. But he has not presented adults as monsters. John's father and mother may have been wrong, but they care, they are conscientious, they have suffered years of worry; and this is clear enough to the perceptive reader, whether adult or child. And in Southall's books the limitations of children are as crucial as those of parents. One of the things the children learn in *Hills End* is that 'one didn't realize how wonderful parents were till they weren't there'. Actually we are *all* only human.

Ivan Southall

Ivan Southall is a strong, masculine writer whose style is direct and active, sometimes staccato. His narratives give the impression of moving at high speed under high pressure. At times, as when the fire draws near in *Ash Road* or the boy Gerald takes over from the dead pilot in *To the Wild Sky*, one feels the surge of adrenalin into the bloodstream. His power is extraordinary. Nevertheless I find him difficult to assess and his progress difficult to forecast. Most novelists probably work within quite a narrow range: often narrower than is realized. But Southall's range at present seems *too* narrow. It is hard to see how he can go on facing more and more groups of characters with catastrophe; how he can go on cranking up the same kind of tension. The force and intensity of his imagination have been fully demonstrated; its breadth remains to be proved. Yet clearly he is a gifted and highly intelligent writer. It seems inevitable that before long he will move in a new direction.

In the course of an article in THE HORN BOOK for June 1968, Ivan Southall wrote:

I woke up one morning in 1960, thirty-nine years of age, determined never to write another book for children. The dear little darlings could go jump in the lake. The thought of producing one more word about my superhero [Simon Black of the Royal Australian Air Force] was more than I could stomach. The sense of relief, of escape, of freedom was bliss indeed.

At the time, I was considering a theme for a novel. I had never written a novel and had never pretended to be a creative writer in the strictest sense, but I was faced with a time delay before I could start in earnest my next documentary, which was to take me to the Woomera Rocket Range; and Woomera was not ready to receive me. As doubtfully endowed as I felt my talent for literary experiment to be, the theme for the novel began to look seriously like a vehicle of the most ordinary kind for children. But I had, after all, sworn off children's books and with my Simon Black mentality had never peopled any book with flesh-and-blood average folk, adults *or* children. For children, I had produced superheroes; for adults, giants, all larger than life. If a subject had failed to attain heroic proportions he had failed also to hold my professional interest.

Now, for the first time, I found myself looking at my own children and their friends growing up round about me. In their lives interacting one upon the other at an unknown depth, I began to suspect with genuine astonishment that here lay an unlimited source of raw material far more exciting than the theme itself. Thus there came a positive moment of decision for me.

Hills End, one of the most exciting adventures of my life, physical or mental, poured out from the first word to last in six weeks, a fraction of the time I had devoted to anything else.

Six to twelve months was the usual run. *Hills End* did not stick to plan and veered far from the predetermined plot; the characters dominated and directed its course. It surprised my fondly respected Australian publishers, not favourably at first. I had to defend it with spirit, and for various reasons publication was delayed for two years. This interminable time convinced me they were printing it only to please me, and discouragement sent me off in other directions. Not until June, 1964, was I free to look seriously at the surprising fact that *Hills End* possessed merit discernible to others and might indicate an area I should examine again . . .

Ash Road came, as *Hills End* had come, clearly and with elation, filled with the excitement of discovering the minds of children and of finding a degree of involvement worth every moment of the months of search. I felt that I had become a child again, that I was writing *out* of my own childhood, and that the standards of maturity were necessary only as a filter of the most superficial kind. *Ash Road* was a raising-up, not a writing-down. It was an appreciation of the vivid colour of childhood, of its heightened reality, of the tensions, impressions, perceptions, toughness and anxieties that the adult forgets and dismisses as ultimately unimportant. Heaven forbid that I should imply that these qualities infuse the book, but they were *my* reward, *my* dividends.

There was also the discovery that truth is more purely expressed through the medium of fiction than it is in works allegedly of fact. A critical discovery far from unique or profound, but something that each writer must learn from life for himself. Writing had always been a fulfilment, but never before, except with *Hills End*, in this particular way.

Hills End, I suppose, was a diversion; but *Ash Road* was the conscious if imperfect beginning of a different professional and private life.

Ivan Southall

Bibliography

Books for children include:

MEET SIMON BLACK. Angus and Robertson, 1950.
SIMON BLACK IN PERIL. Angus and Robertson, 1951.
SIMON BLACK IN SPACE. Angus and Robertson, 1952.
SIMON BLACK IN COASTAL COMMAND. Angus and Robertson, 1953.
SIMON BLACK IN CHINA. Angus and Robertson, 1954.
SIMON BLACK AND THE SPACEMEN. Angus and Robertson, 1955.
SIMON BLACK IN THE ANTARCTIC. Angus and Robertson, 1956.
SIMON BLACK TAKES OVER. Angus and Robertson, 1959.
SIMON BLACK AT SEA. Angus and Robertson, 1961.
JOURNEY INTO MYSTERY. Lansdowne-Angus and Robertson, 1961.
HILL'S END. Angus and Robertson, 1962; St Martin's Press, 1963.
ROCKETS IN THE DESERT. Angus and Robertson, 1964.
ASH ROAD. Angus and Robertson, 1965; St Martin's Press, 1965.
INDONESIAN JOURNEY. Lansdowne-Angus and Robertson, 1965; Ginn, 1966.
TO THE WILD SKY. Angus and Robertson, 1967; St Martin's Press, 1967.
THE FOX HOLE. Methuen, 1967; St Martin's Press, 1967.
THE SWORD OF ESAU. Angus and Robertson, 1967; St Martin's Press, 1968.
LET THE BALLOON GO. Methuen, 1968; St Martin's Press, 1968.
THE CURSE OF CAIN. Angus and Robertson, 1968; St Martin's Press, 1968.
THE SLY OLD WARDROBE. Cheshire-Angus and Robertson, 1968; St Martin's Press, 1970.
FINN'S FOLLY. Angus and Robertson, 1969; St Martin's Press, 1969.
CHINAMAN'S REEF IS OURS. Angus and Robertson, 1970; St Martin's Press, 1970.
BREAD AND HONEY. Angus and Robertson, 1970; Bradbury Press, 1970, as WALK A MILE AND GET NOWHERE.

Rosemary Sutcliff

Rosemary Sutcliff was born in 1920, the daughter of a naval officer. Since she was two years old she has suffered from a poly-arthritic condition which has restricted her physical movement. She first went to school when she was nine, and left 'mercifully early' at fourteen. She trained to be a painter, but turned to writing when she was in her twenties. She has now published more than a score of books, of which the best known are her historical novels for children and young people. Among these are several set in Britain during and after the Roman occupation, including the sequence consisting of The Eagle of the Ninth *(1954),* The Silver Branch *(1957), and* The Lantern Bearers, *winner of the Carnegie Medal for 1959.*

Day to day, minute to minute, second to second the surface of our lives is in a perpetual ripple of change. Below the immediate surface are slower, deeper currents, and below these again are profound mysterious movements beyond the scale of the individual life-span. And far down on the sea-bed are the oldest, most lasting things, whose changes our imagination can hardly grasp at all. The strength of Rosemary Sutcliff's main work—and it is a body of work rather than a shelf of novels—is its sense of movement on all these scales. Bright the surface may be, and vigorous the action of the moment, but it is never detached from the forces underneath that give it meaning. She puts more into the reader's consciousness than he is immediately aware of.

She is not—in terms of the novel in general rather than of the children's list—a fashionable writer, or even very well known. She is not, for instance, mentioned at all in Anthony Burgess's *The Novel Now*, a 'student's guide to contemporary fiction' which was published in 1967, although many authors are discussed whose talents are far slighter than hers. It may be that Miss Sutcliff's virtues are not fundamentally a novelist's virtues.

The novel is much more concerned with individual character and day-to-day living than were the ancient forms that came before it. Rosemary Sutcliff's work is rooted more in myth, legend and saga than in the English novel.

She was a slow starter. The promise of her early books was not outstanding. *The Queen Elizabeth Story* (1950), *The Armourer's House* (1951) and *Brother Dusty-Feet* (1952) were innocuous, episodic historical stories for quite young children of perhaps eight to eleven. The backgrounds were already solid, and the storytelling, as distinct from story-construction, was already effective. In each case the story covers a period of many months, and the chapters are strung like beads on a thread; they do not often arise out of each other. Perdita, who longs to see the great Queen, and Tamsyn, who goes to live with her cousins in the bustling house of her uncle the armourer, are nice little girls; Hugh, who runs away from his unpleasant aunt to tramp the dusty lanes, is a brave, sturdy boy; but there is no real life in any of them. The atmosphere is almost cosy; as it is, too, in the retold *Chronicles of Robin Hood*, published in 1950. The England of Elizabeth I is suspiciously close to being that of Good Queen Bess. The tone of voice is sometimes condescending, and simplicity can sink into naïvety or be misleading, as, for instance, in the presentation of the life of a company of strolling players as one of innocent good-fellowship.

Simon (1953) has an English Civil War setting and is a transitional book. Miss Sutcliff is writing for an older age-group and with more complexity. The action, as in so many later books, is spread over several years. *Simon* is not to my mind a success. It gives the impression that a good deal of military history has been imperfectly transposed into fiction; the conflict of loyalties in a friendship that cuts across the civil-war lines is rather obvious, and the hero a dull fellow. The sub-theme of Corporal Zeal-for-the-Lord Relf, consumed with a passion for vengeance on the man who robbed him of thirty pounds and his double white hyacinth, is much more disturbing, and comes more strongly to life, than the main one.

And then, after these tentative beginnings, Miss Sutcliff's big C-major theme comes in with *The Eagle of the Ninth* (1954). This book is perhaps more of a complete novel, more satisfying in itself, than any other of her books so far; yet at the same time it is the first stage in a complex construction of which a great deal of her later work can be said to form part.

There are three 'Roman novels', the second and third being *The Silver Branch* (1957) and *The Lantern Bearers* (1959); but the break between the Roman books and their successors really comes early in *The Lantern Bearers*, when the galleys leave Britain and the hero, Aquila, though a Roman citizen and officer, decides to stay in the small benighted island where he was born. The theme, as Margaret Meek pointed out in her Bodley Head monograph on Rosemary Sutcliff, is 'the light and the dark'. In *The Lantern Bearers* the light is carried, weak and guttering, into the darkness. The events of this book are followed by those of the adult novel *Sword at Sunset* (1963) where Arthur is presented as a British war leader fighting a doomed rearguard action against the invading hordes. In *Dawn Wind* (1961) the theme and the metaphor are extended; there is not only 'the last gleam of a lantern far behind', but there is also 'the hope of other light as far ahead' in the prospect of a union of Briton and Saxon in the Christian faith.

But 'the light and the dark' is not the only theme; nor does it cover all that the author thinks and feels about civilization and barbarism. An overriding subject, extended over many books, is the making of Britain. This goes back to the Bronze Age in *Warrior Scarlet* (1958); and forward to *The Shield Ring* (1956), in which Norseman meets Norman, and *Knight's Fee* (1960), where the Norman Conquest is over and Normans too are beginning to lose themselves in a common identity. And Miss Sutcliff moves sideways, as it were, from Roman Britain in *The Mark of the Horse Lord* (1965), in which Phaedrus the Gladiator first impersonates, then becomes identified with, the leader of the Gaelic 'horse people'. Peoples mix, conquerors are absorbed, and all along, timeless and patient, from *Warrior Scarlet* right through to *Knight's Fee* two thousand years later, are the Little Dark People, who endure and survive.

Miss Sutcliff's link with Kipling – especially of *Puck of Pook's Hill* – is well known and acknowledged, and in this theme of continuity it is seen at its strongest. Continuity is emphasized by the recurrence of symbolic objects: the flawed emerald ring in the Roman novels, and in *Sword at Sunset* and *Dawn Wind*; the silver branch in the book to which it gives its name and also in *Sword at Sunset* and *The Mark of the Horse Lord*; the weathered flint axe-head, found on the Downs, that links Randal in *Knight's Fee* with Drem, right back in *Warrior Scarlet*.

And 'the light and the dark' is not a division between good and bad. Just as Kipling, a man of the West, could respect and appreciate the different values of the East (see especially *Kim*), so Miss Sutcliff, who strikes me as a rather Roman writer herself, can understand qualities which from a Roman point of view might be called barbarian. Here, a passage from *The Eagle of the Ninth* is crucial. Esca, the former clansman, now companion of the Roman hero Marcus, shows him a shield-boss:

> 'See the bulging curves that flow from each other as water flows from water and wind from wind, as the stars turn in the heavens and blown sand drifts into dunes. These are the curves of life; and the man who traced them had in him knowledge of things that your people have lost the key to–if they ever had it. . . . You are the builders of coursed stone walls, the makers of straight roads and ordered justice and disciplined troops. We know that, we know it all too well. We know that your justice is more sure than ours, and when we rise against you, we see our hosts break against the discipline of your troops, as the sea breaks against a rock. And we do not understand, because all these things are of the ordered pattern, and only the free curves of the shield-boss are real to us.

The last great Sutcliff theme, again running through all the major books, is at the most basic level of all. This is death and rebirth as a condition of the continuance of life. Appropriately, this is most explicit in *Warrior Scarlet*, the earliest book in its subject-matter. Here it recurs perpetually: in the rites of king-making, the boys who die as boys to be reborn as warriors, the killing of the Corn King, the New Fire and the young men and girls who leap through it at Beltane. In *The Mark of the Horse Lord*, among those who follow the Old Way, the King must die every seven years. The death of Arthur in *Sword at Sunset* is recounted in a chapter of which 'The Corn King' is the unexplained but significant title. In *Knight's Fee*, whose setting is Norman England, the old rites are still not far below the surface.

A further preoccupation of Miss Sutcliff, which gives her books their special relevance for young people but nevertheless goes far beyond any such sectional appeal, is that of the proving of the hero. This theme recurs so often that I need not link it with a succession of titles. It seems to me that this is part of the major theme just mentioned. It is necessary to come through a testing ordeal in order to die as a boy—or unproved man—and be reborn as man and warrior. Nearly all Miss Sutcliff's heroes are warriors. They are also leaders, and two of them are, for practical purposes, kings. Leadership has its price, and the greater the leadership the greater the price. It is the duty and privilege and ultimate glory of a king to die that his people may flourish. So die Arthur in *Sword at Sunset* and Phaedrus in *The Mark of the Horse Lord*. We are in the shadow of the Golden Bough.

Where there is a body of linked work on themes of this size it seems unusually difficult, and is perhaps less than usually meaningful, to attempt assessments of individual books. Physically, of course, they are separate novels, likely to be approached within the unconscious frame of reference that we erect for a novel. This may be why the single books which I personally like best tend to be those which stand up well on their own: *Warrior Scarlet* and *Knight's Fee*, which come at the beginning and end of the time-span of Miss Sutcliff's major work, and *The Eagle of the Ninth* and *The Mark of the Horse Lord*, which again have their intrinsic shapes and feel complete in themselves. The other Roman and post-Roman books seem to me to contain so much strife and confusion, to cover so many years and so much ground, that although impressive as parts of a wider design they fail to fit the novel form; it cannot hold them. Least satisfactory of all I find *Sword at Sunset*, which was not originally published on a children's list, although it has since appeared in an abridged version in Peacock books, the Penguin series for adolescent readers. Here the incorporation of legendary material into the historical framework has been achieved at the cost of nearly all its vitality. Arthur, or Artos, has become a standard Sutcliff warrior, and even then is not convincing as narrator; and Miss

Sutcliff's Guenhumara is a feeble figure beside the Guinevere of legend.

Although it is not too difficult to find differences among Rosemary Sutcliff's heroes, they nevertheless seem to me to be from the same mould. They are brave but not reckless, thoughtful but limited, conscientious, reliable, true to their friends, stiff-upper-lipped. They face and overcome their difficulties, though not with ease. They are not gay or dashing; they suggest the Service officer rather than the independent adventurer, or—however humble their origins may be—the common man. They are not artists, and one feels that although they would try dutifully to appreciate the worth of the artist they would never enter his world. There is a revealing sentence at the end of *Knight's Fee* when the minstrel Herluin, though indebted to the hero Randal for his freedom, thinks it 'more than likely' that he would find life dull with Randal on his Downland manor. The reader may well agree. Some of the Sutcliff heroes are unexciting, though worthy. And their concern with the achievement of adult status and the respect of their peers may appear out of tune with the present time, when some of the liveliest young people are deliberately rejecting the standards of the adult world and saying that they don't want to be accepted into it anyway. (This of course may be a temporary phenomenon, and less widespread than it sometimes appears, and in any case it is no reflection on Miss Sutcliff's work.)

The fiery girls who make up Miss Sutcliff's little band of feminine characters are thinly sketched, and only just exist as people. Her villains, major and minor, come straight from stock; her most notable successes in characterization may well be her tetchy old men. She rarely practises the novelist's art of building up tension towards a single climax, and she is not above making excessive use of coincidence.

Yet there can be few writers who cope anything like so well as she does with the passage of time, who can speed or slow up the narrative so effortlessly as it leaves or arrives at its significant points. Miss Sutcliff's writing is highly pictorial. At the same time she has a splendid gift for the stirring account of swift action, and she can combine these qualities most effectively. In *The Mark of the Horse Lord*, an account of preparations for the ritual killing of the horse people's king continues for several pages: unhurried, holding the attention by the strength of its colour and atmosphere, yet with a growing sense of imminent storm, for we know that an uprising has been planned for this occasion. Then, suddenly, fighting breaks out, and a minute or two later

> ... from somewhere in the heart of the Dun, a tongue of flame leapt up, blurred and wavering in the mist. Men were pouring through the great gate that had been opened to them, swarming in over the ramparts, men who carried each a spare weapon with him. Phaedrus with one such sword in his hand, Conory racing beside him with his own again, were storming forward at the head of a swelling band against the main mass of the Queen's party ...
>
> Another band of men and women, headed by the wild figure of Logiore with his horse-mane flying, came charging in across their path. They also were fully armed, for by now weapons were springing into every hand; and in the light of scattered fires and guttering torches Phaedrus thought he glimpsed in the midst of the battle-throng around the gateway the moon-silver gleam of the Queen's diadem.

Miss Sutcliff, according to a reviewer quoted in Margaret Meek's monograph, 'will always put down her harp for a battle'. But her most obvious gift of all is what Miss Meek correctly describes as 'the total imaginative penetration of the historical material'. There is a great deal of violent action in her books, but it is never meaningless violence, violence for violence's sake, violence that in the end defeats itself and deadens the reader's response. Always one has a sense of what it is all about. At the same time there is little that is abstract, and there are no painstaking and lifeless reconstructions. For Rosemary Sutcliff the past is not something to be taken down from the shelf and dusted. It comes out of her pages alive and breathing and now.

Rosemary Sutcliff writes:

It seems incredible, when I stop to think about it, that I have been writing books, mostly children's though a few adults', for more than twenty years. The day the letter arrived from Oxford University Press accepting *The Queen Elizabeth Story* still seems so near and vivid, and yet a little as though it had happened to somebody else. When, for one reason or another, I dip into one of my early books, it's as though they had been written by somebody else, too.

And they all seem to have been written so easily. They don't only seem, they *were* written so easily. In those early days I didn't know how hard it was to write books—at least books that satisfy the deep inner inquiring something in oneself—and so I embarked on them with complete lightheartedness, and they simply 'came'. I was a little like the bumblebee. The bumblebee, so I have been told, has according to all the laws of aerodynamics insufficient wing-power to become airborne, but nobody has told the bumblebee this, and so it flies around quite happily. Nobody in those days had told me about the strains and stresses of creating; I learned them for myself as time—and books—went by and I became more and more aware of what was entailed. I think one of the troubles is that with each book one becomes more and more of a perfectionist (and perfectionists do not always produce the best results) and also perhaps one feels the need to go deeper and deeper into one's subject. (The characterization, the motivation, the ethos of *The Mark of the Horse Lord* are very far removed from those of *The Eagle of the Ninth*, which is still, alas, my favourite among my own books.) One can't stop this process any more than one can stop growth or undo an experience. I suppose that's why my books have tended over the years to be written for older and older age-groups, or rather, to have appealed to older and older age-groups, because I have never written for any age-group at all, but merely for myself.

That, also, is why it's a relief to write an occasional adult book, though I should hate to switch to adult books altogether. The themes of my children's books are mostly quite adult, and in fact the difference between writing for children and for adults is, to me at any rate, only a quite small gear-change. But there are problems in writing officially for children, certain subjects that have to be treated carefully even when they are not altogether tabu, for the sake of publishers, librarians and parents rather than for the children themselves: motives and relationships that have to be a little simplified. And so in some ways it is harder to write a children's book than an adults', and it can be enlarging to take a deep breath now and then and, knowing that there are no holds barred, embark on a book such as *Sword at Sunset* or *The Flowers of Adonis*.

Rosemary Sutcliff

Bibliography

Books for children

THE CHRONICLES OF ROBIN HOOD. Oxford University Press, 1950.
THE QUEEN ELIZABETH STORY. Oxford University Press, 1950.
THE ARMOURER'S HOUSE. Oxford University Press, 1951.
BROTHER DUSTY-FEET. Oxford University Press, 1952.
SIMON. Oxford University Press, 1953.
THE EAGLE OF THE NINTH. Oxford University Press, 1954; Walck, 1954.
OUTCAST. Oxford University Press, 1955; Walck, 1955.
THE SHIELD RING. Oxford University Press, 1956; Walck, 1957.
THE SILVER BRANCH. Oxford University Press, 1957; Walck, 1958.
WARRIOR SCARLET. Oxford University Press, 1958; Walck, 1958.
THE LANTERN BEARERS. Oxford University Press, 1959; Walck, 1959.
HOUSES AND HISTORY. Batsford, 1960.
KNIGHT'S FEE. Oxford University Press, 1960; Walck, 1960.
RUDYARD KIPLING. The Bodley Head, 1960; Walck, 1961.
BEOWULF. The Bodley Head, 1961; Dutton, 1962.
DAWN WIND. Oxford University Press, 1961; Walck, 1962.
THE HOUND OF ULSTER. The Bodley Head, 1963; Dutton, 1964.
HEROES AND HISTORY. Batsford, 1965; Putnam, 1966.
THE MARK OF THE HORSE LORD. Oxford University Press, 1965; Walck, 1965.
A SAXON SETTLER. Oxford University Press (*People of the Past series*), 1965.
THE CHIEF'S DAUGHTER. Hamish Hamilton, 1967; Dutton, 1971.
THE HIGH DEEDS OF FINN MAC COOL. The Bodley Head, 1967; Dutton, 1967.
A CIRCLET OF OAK LEAVES. Hamish Hamilton, 1968; Dutton, 1971.
THE WITCH'S BRAT. Oxford University Press, 1970; Walck, 1970.
TRISTAN AND ISEULT. The Bodley Head, 1971.
THE TRUCE OF THE GAMES. Hamish Hamilton, 1971; Dutton, 1971.

Rosemary Sutcliff

In addition to the books for children listed above, two of Rosemary Sutcliff's novels for adults, THE RIDER OF THE WHITE HORSE and SWORD AT SUNSET, have been published for young people in abridged editions (Peacock Books, 1964 and 1965).

Rosemary Sutcliff's short stories for children include *The Bridge-Builders* in ANOTHER SIX (Blackwell, 1959), *The Fugitives* in MISCELLANY ONE, edited by Edward Blishen (Oxford University Press, 1964), *The Man Who Died at Sea* in THE HOUSE OF THE NIGHTMARE AND OTHER EERIE TALES, edited by Kathleen Lines (The Bodley Head, 1967; Farrar, Straus and Giroux, 1968), *The Making of an Outlaw* in THRILLING STORIES FROM THE PAST FOR BOYS, edited by Eric Duthie (Odhams Press, 1970) and *Swallows in the Spring* in GALAXY, edited by Gabrielle Maunder (Oxford University Press, 1970).

Patricia Wrightson

Patricia Wrightson was born in Lismore, New South Wales, Australia, in 1921. She received part of her education through the State Correspondence School, which gives lessons by post to children who live in remote places. For several years she worked in hospital management; now she is on the editorial staff of the New South Wales Department of Education's School Magazine. *She is divorced and has a grown-up son and daughter. Among her novels are* The Rocks of Honey *(1960),* The Feather Star *(1962),* Down to Earth *(1965), and* 'I Own the Racecourse!' *(1968).*

Patricia Wrightson published her first novel in 1955. She is not prolific, and twelve years later she had produced only four more books. By then she had built up a modest reputation as an intelligent and perceptive regional writer, but outside Australia her name was still not widely known. Then in 1968 came '*I Own the Racecourse!*' (in America *A Racecourse for Andy*), a story about a backward boy who 'buys' a city racetrack for three dollars and insists on taking a share in running it. It was highly successful, both with children and with adult reviewers, and Mrs Wrightson was suddenly recognized as a leading children's writer.

The success of '*I Own the Racecourse!*' was well deserved, and seems less surprising when one looks back with hindsight on the books that led up to it. As often happens, Mrs Wrightson had displayed qualities individually in previous books which only needed to be drawn together. *The Rocks of Honey* (1960) had shown an exceptional imaginative range and a willingness to tackle large and difficult themes. *The Feather Star*—Mrs Wrightson's most feminine novel, published in 1962—was remarkable for the sensitivity and precision of its character-drawing, while *Down to Earth* in 1965 gave play to a bold comic imagination and a gift for making ideas interesting. Together these three should have indicated that something far out of the ordinary might now be expected.

Besides combining the special qualities of its immediate predecessors, '*I Own the Racecourse!*' shares with all Patricia Wrightson's previous work the benefit of a talent for managing a largish cast of children or young people and bringing them to life both as individuals and in group relationships. In addition, Mrs Wrightson has an unusually strong sense of place. Her stories are notable for the solidity of their settings: the New South Wales bush for the first three; a little seaside resort for *The Feather Star*; the city of Sydney, bustling, various and almost tangible, for the fifth and sixth.

Mrs Wrightson's first two books, *The Crooked Snake* (1955) and *The Bunyip Hole* (1958) have been out of print for some years and are now difficult to find. *The Crooked Snake* is about a group of boys and girls who form a society, set out with cameras on a holiday project, and find themselves in conflict with destructive older schoolfellows. The theme of *The Bunyip Hole* is superficially similar; the Collins children, picnicking and camping beside a natural pool which they wish to clear for summer use, are harried by a couple of older boys they call the Ring-Tailed Bandicoots. But here the most important happenings are those that take place within the Collins family, and particularly inside young Binty, a timid boy with too much imagination for his own comfort. Binty – who understandably detests his given name of Herbert – sets out full of apprehension to rescue his dog Homer from the Bandicoots and finishes up trapped with Homer on a ledge with a chasm beneath him; his rescue is due to his own painfully-mustered courage as well as the efforts of his resourceful older brother and sister.

The Bunyip Hole is a pleasing story but much more limited in scope than its successor, *The Rocks of Honey*, which begins in a matter-of-fact way but goes on to open up some unexpected perspectives. The main characters are a trio of children: Barney, the practical son of a farmer; Eustace, an amiable aboriginal boy who responds to every suggestion with a cheerful 'I don't mind'; and Winnie, a disconcertingly silent, independent and unpredictable small girl. The two boys become engaged in a quest for an ancient stone axe, reputed to lie hidden among the group of rocks now known as the Three Sisters but formerly the Rocks of Honey. It is a pleasantly casual quest, the excuse for a good deal of exploring and picnicking and den-making; and then the story suddenly takes off, with the interpolation of a chapter telling how, long years ago, Warrimai the club-thrower made the axe, and how he came to put it, with a curse upon it, among these rocks. And when the axe comes directly into the story, tension rises and persists.

In the midst of a storm the axe is found—by Winnie, not by the boys. Eustace and his uncle, as aboriginals, are convinced that it should be put back where it came from. Barney thinks this is nonsense. But soon the axe is the cause of three strange accidents, one after the other. Perhaps they are only coincidence, but still . . . Barney and Winnie now agree that the axe should go back. And, replacing it among the Rocks of Honey, Eustace hears in the wind the Song of the Old King:

> . . . Oh, my country, the warm land of the Honey,
> Have you broken and thrown away your own brown people?

The underlying theme, it becomes clear, is a weighty one: the changing relationship of the land and the two peoples. And the author has sought to indicate the different ways of thought and feeling of the brown people and the white. Between Barney and Eustace, who have never felt any racial antipathy, the quest for the axe brings a believable strangeness. The different moods of the story reflect a similar duality. In the second half there is nothing explicitly supernatural, but there is a pervading sense of old magic, an awareness that there could be more in heaven and earth than practical farmers' sons normally think of. *The Rocks of Honey* is not entirely successful; its transitions are sometimes awkward, and the author may have reached out for more than she could grasp at that stage of her development; but it is an impressive story, and comes to seem more so at a second and third reading. On the more workaday of its two levels, the relationship of the three children is well handled, and at least one cliché-situation is blessedly avoided. In this trio it is Winnie who is the wistful outsider, because she is a girl, not Eustace because he is an aboriginal.

Patricia Wrightson

The Feather Star is the story of a girl's farewell to childhood, of the beginnings of her growing up. This is a familiar subject which can easily be boring or embarrassing; but Mrs Wrightson doesn't put a foot wrong. Fifteen-year-old Lindy, on an out-of-season family holiday at the seaside, is burdened with small brother Chris and Chris's tiresome friend Annie Tippett. ('Go on home, Annie Tippett' is the automatic reaction to Annie's appearance in any gathering.) And even when she gets a few minutes on her own, Lindy doesn't quite know who she is. One time she wanders along the beach and picks up shells:

> Soon she had collected three pink, glittering shells, a delicate blue one, a twisty bit of driftwood like a snake, a fan-shaped sponge and a lump of pumice. She gathered them with the same small excitement with which she had gathered other hoards like this, year by year since she was tiny; and now, all at once, the excitement went out of them. What would she do with these things if she took them home? . . . She put them all down on a stone so that she could forget them without actually throwing them away, and went to sit on the rocks at the end of the wall.

With the girl who works in the shop – Felice, pronounced Fleece – and two boys she forms a tentative foursome: shy, teasing, self-conscious, not knowing what to say to each other. The feather star of the title is a sea creature found by Lindy in a cave; broken, it will grow again two or threefold, and it symbolizes – one assumes – the breakup of childhood. Interestingly, Lindy's loss of childish innocence comes not in any of the obvious ways but through a series of encounters with a dreadful, censorious, all-hating old man. There is no reconciliation with him, because he is lost, irredeemably lost, and the realization that this can happen is a fearful thing. 'She sobbed and sobbed, child and woman together, for the tragedy and wickedness of Abel. She sobbed for useless misery and bitterness; for age with its eyes on the ground refusing life, wasting all the adventure and beauty of a whirling planet in space.'

The adventure and beauty of a whirling planet in space. Add courage and humour and you have – as Mrs Wrightson herself says – the theme of *Down to Earth*. This is a strange fantasy, set in the streets of Sydney and opened and closed by the arrival and departure of 'Martin the Martian'. It is not science-fiction; it is in part a look at life here as it might seem to an intelligent visitor from another world—an idea which goes back at least to the Persian Letters of Montesquieu in the early eighteenth century, though Persia is no longer far enough away. Not only is there the question of how we look to an outside observer; there is the question of what we would *do* about such an observer if we became aware of him.

To George and Cathy, who find him living in an empty house, Martin looks like an ordinary boy. He tries to explain it to them:

> 'You think you can see me, but you can't really; because I'm quite outside the range of what your brain was built to see. But your mind realizes there's another mind there, a sort of person, so your mind makes the picture it always does make for that sort of thing and you think you're really seeing me. To you I just look like an Earth person, because that's the only sort your brain can see.'
>
> 'I get it,' said George encouragingly. 'And what about when you look at us?'
>
> 'The same thing,' said the boy. It seemed to annoy him a little to admit it. 'To me you look just like us.'
>
> 'What, space men?' demanded George, immensely tickled. 'Are we purple? Have we got horns?'
>
> 'It's no use asking, can't you understand? We can't even tell each other. Our minds can only take in what they can understand. I say you're not purple with horns and you say you're not purple with horns, and we think we're saying the same thing, but perhaps we each mean something different.'

Martin loves to watch crowds in motion. At the zoo he is, predictably, found 'with his back to the cages, laughing gleefully in the wrong direction'. He is surprised by the sport of fishing:

> 'I should have thought that if an Earth man wanted a fish he would jump into the sea and stab one; or drop a small bomb and blow up a quantity; or find some way of dragging out of the sea several tons of fish to choose from.'

'They do all these things too,' George admitted. 'But except for this way and spear-fishing, it's not really sport. Doesn't give the fish a fighting chance.'

'Ah!' cried Martin, beginning to understand. 'The fish must fight, too. I see.'

It is doubtful whether Martin is 'a boy' in his own society, or whether the idea would mean anything there, but George and Cathy look on him as a boy and feel protective towards him. And Martin needs protection, for, however intelligent, he is quite guileless, unequipped with the self-preservatory cunning that we all need in the civilized jungle we inhabit. In fact, as the author presents him, he *is* a boy: a nice, amenable and slightly vain one. When he falls into the well-meaning hands of the Child Welfare Department, George and Cathy know they must rescue him and keep him out of the way of authority until he can catch a ship back to wherever he came from. All in all, this is a slight but far from feeble story which pokes mildly satirical fun in several directions. It is totally different from the two that preceded it; and its successor is totally different again.

The boys in '*I Own the Racecourse!*' play the game of 'buying' and swapping property. Andy is the 'slow' one who doesn't quite understand, who goes to a separate school. And Andy outdoes all the rest, for their deals are only pretended but *he* thinks he's really bought the racecourse with the three dollars he paid to a tramp. The men who work there humour Andy and call him 'boss'. And the whole thing inflates itself alarmingly, with Andy becoming happily and innocently famous all over the district as the racecourse-owner.

A frequent Wrightson sub-theme – taken straight from life, and not over-used in modern children's fiction – is that of the sense of responsibility which older children will accept for younger or weaker ones. Andy's friends Joe and Mike care about him, stick up for him, look after him; but now they are in conflict. Joe is worried over Andy's delusion: 'He's getting in deeper all the time. He's got to come out of it.' Mike sees it differently; the episode is doing Andy a power of good, and since he can go where he wants, do what he wants, and be generally treated as the owner, why then, for the present he *does* own the racecourse.

Whichever is right, the thing must end some time, for Andy cannot spend the rest of his life in a magnificent dream. There are practical reasons, too, why it has to stop; for Andy, though a mascot to the men, becomes an increasing nuisance to the racecourse's management. One wonders what way out there can be that will not deal a fearful psychological blow to Andy. But the author finds one; and it is the perfect and satisfying answer. A truly original plot is just about the rarest thing in fiction; '*I Own the Racecourse!*' has one.

As Mrs Wrightson asks, how real is reality? For that matter, what is ownership? The land and buildings of the racecourse are nothing; its true existence is only in action, especially when the trotting races are on in the great illuminated stadium:

> With a rustling and drumming the horses sprang into view, spread wide across the track. Powerful, beating fore-legs, deep, straining chests and rolling eyes, they hurtled along the track straight at the boys. The three of them hung silent and breathless on the rails with the crowd packed round them. The voice from the amplifiers chanted on . . . Cockaded heads high, the fierce horses passed. The drivers in their shining satin were perched above whirling wheels. The horses swung towards the inner rail and flowed in a dark stream round the curve . . .
>
> Round the track again, and a string of red lights flashed as they passed the big stand. The amplified voice grew frenzied and was almost drowned by the roaring of the crowd. They went by like dark thunder, whips flashing and drivers' faces grim; and round the track the roar of the crowd travelled with them. This time a white light flashed, and the horses went flying separately, slowing and turning one by one. The race was over.

Nobody can 'own' this any more than Andy. And although like 'Martin the Martian' Andy is poorly equipped for the business of daily life, he is surely something more than is implied by words like 'simple' or 'backward'. Could it be that, like Martin, he has something the fully-equipped, earthbound person lacks?

'*I Own the Racecourse!*' offers, besides a well-told and ingenious story, a new way of looking at things for those who want and are ready for it. It is because of this freshness of eye, together with her interest in ideas and her readiness to introduce something different and out-of-the-ordinary into each successive book, that Patricia Wrightson is such a stimulating writer.

Of course one does not expect the majority of children – or adults – to stop and think about the issues a story may raise. Most of us read fiction for pleasure, and there is nothing wrong with that. Yet the book that is exhausted on superficial reading is a bad one almost by definition, whereas a sense that there is more than meets the eye will often emerge half-consciously to enrich the experience of reading. One of the tests of a good novel is that it leaves one with the feeling that there is more to be discovered on further acquaintance. Patricia Wrightson's last four books are all of the kind that are worth coming back to, the kind that linger and echo in the reader's mind.

Patricia Wrightson writes:

I was one of those children of whom a long list of schoolteachers predict that they will grow up to become writers. I left school with the sort of imagination that produces stories, the eye for people that produces a novelist, the feel for words that makes it exhilarating to use them – and no idea what to do about it all; thoroughly intimidated by the excellence of the work already done, and aware that there was nothing in me worth offering to other people. This uneasy and helpless frustration held me until I had children old enough to read, when it occurred to me that if I, as a mother, had nothing worth saying to children, the outlook for my own children was pretty poor. And in fact I did find plenty to say to *them*. So I ventured to try my hand at a novel for children, very deliberately making my work into a course of training; requiring that in each book I should break new and (for me) difficult ground, and hoping to graduate to adult novels some day.

I still hope to do so – when I have come to the end of this field, and goodness knows when that will be. I think that I, as a potential writer, was immensely lucky to stumble into the field of novels for children. There could be no better, stricter or more demanding discipline. Nowhere is artificiality, or the intrusion of ego, more instantly obvious. Nowhere is economy, and therefore precision, more demanded. The writer who is offering his ideas to other people's children has a heavy obligation to be sure of their validity and his own sincerity. It is often not good enough to say, as one may to one's own children, 'Well, I think so, anyway,' and go on to offer a one-sided argument. Also, if you want an idea to be comprehensible at all you must think it right through to its roots, when it often turns out to be something too trite to be worth saying. In an adult novel, woolly and pretentious thinking may fool readers and even writers into a belief in the profundity of an idea. Your ideas can't be woolly or pretentious in a novel for children.

You will have gathered that I like themes involving some mental exploration and a stretching of understanding. I may be peculiar in my treatment of them. Having discovered such a theme and worked it out fully, I don't like to write a story that demonstrates it with all the flat-footed authority of an adult backed up by print. I may be wrong; and anyway it seems to me a greater and more important achievement to induce a child to think about it for himself and reach his own conclusions. I have confidence in the ability of children's unscarred minds. It seems to me that if my theme provides *me* with a light by which to write my story, the story will reflect this light and will probably set children thinking for themselves, spontaneously. If, as often happens, adult reviewers don't catch the reflected light, it doesn't worry me too seriously. They read by the light of their own ideas, and their minds are not as sensitive as children's. I believe very few adults may have caught the reflected light of my themes for *Down to Earth* and *'I Own the Racecourse!'*, for instance: in the first, the endearing simplicity of man, clinging to his bit of stardust in space, so certain of his conclusions about things he can only glimpse; the second, the question 'How real is reality anyway?' I still hope that a greater proportion of child readers may have found themselves wondering about these things.

Patricia Wrightson

Bibliography

THE CROOKED SNAKE. Angus and Robertson, 1955.
THE BUNYIP HOLE. Angus and Robertson, 1957.
THE ROCKS OF HONEY. Angus and Robertson, 1960.
THE FEATHER STAR. Hutchinson, 1962; Harcourt Brace, 1963.
DOWN TO EARTH. Hutchinson, 1965; Harcourt Brace, 1968.
'I OWN THE RACECOURSE!' Hutchinson, 1968; Harcourt Brace, 1968, as A RACECOURSE FOR ANDY.

A Note About the Author

John Rowe Townsend was born in Leeds and attended the grammar school there. At Cambridge he took an honours degree in English and edited the university newspaper. He worked as a journalist on several national newspapers before becoming a sub-editor of *The Manchester Guardian* in 1949 and, subsequently, editor of *The Guardian*'s weekly international edition. He now devotes his time to writing, reviewing and lecturing on children's books.

Mr Townsend is himself a distinguished writer of books for young people. His novels include *Hell's Edge*, which was a runner-up for the Carnegie Medal in 1963, and *The Intruder*, which in 1970 received a Silver Pen award from the English Centre of International P.E.N. and won the Boston Globe-Horn Book award for excellence in text in 1970. His interest in the social conditions of children suggested the themes of *Gumble's Yard* and *Widdershins Crescent* while his particular interest in books for adolescents resulted in *Good-night, Prof, Love*. In addition to fiction for children, Mr Townsend has written an historical study of English children's literature, *Written For Children*. His reviews and writings on children's books appear regularly in *The Guardian* and elsewhere.

John Rowe Townsend's books include:

GUMBLE'S YARD. Hutchinson, 1961; Lippincott, 1969, as TROUBLE IN THE JUNGLE.

HELL'S EDGE. Hutchinson, 1963; Lothrop, 1969.

WIDDERSHINS CRESCENT. Hutchinson, 1965; Lippincott, 1967, as GOOD-BYE TO THE JUNGLE.

THE HALLERSAGE SOUND. Hutchinson, 1966.

WRITTEN FOR CHILDREN: AN OUTLINE OF ENGLISH CHILDREN'S LITERATURE. Garnet Miller, 1965; Lothrop, 1967.

PIRATE'S ISLAND. Oxford University Press, 1968; Lippincott, 1968.
THE INTRUDER. Oxford University Press, 1969; Lippincott, 1970.
GOOD-NIGHT, PROF, LOVE. Oxford University Press, 1970; Lippincott, 1971.
A WISH FOR WINGS. Heinemann, 1971.

John Rowe Townsend contributed the title story to THE FRIDAY MIRACLE AND OTHER STORIES, edited by Kaye Webb (Puffin Books, 1969) and the introduction to a new edition of ERIC, OR LITTLE BY LITTLE, by Frederic W. Farrar (Hamish Hamilton, 1971). Two essays, on *The Present State of English Children's Literature* and *Didacticism in Modern Dress*, were included in ONLY CONNECT, edited by Sheila Egoff, G. T. Stubbs and L. F. Ashley (Oxford University Press, 1969).